COINCIDENCES

Reflections of the First Black Female Graduate of the United States Naval Academy

Janie L. Mines, USNA '80

Copyright Janie Louvenia Mines © 2019
Reg.#TX 8-673-134

All rights reserved. No part of this book may be used or reproduced by any means, graphic, electronic, or mechanical, including photocopying, recording, taping or by any information storage retrieval system without written permission from the author except in the case of brief quotations embodied in critical articles and reviews.

Published by Custom Messages, Inc., Fort Mill, SC 29715 by arrangement with Janie L. Mines.

Editing by JHwriting+

www.jhwritingplus.com

ISBN 10: 0-692-18249-7
ISBN-13: 978-0-692-18249-9

Library of Congress Control Number
2018911338

From the Yard

Janie Mines applies the religious themes taught by her family in a real-world exposé of how those childhood experiences prepared her to enter the class of 1980 at the U.S. Naval Academy. She reveals a painful chapter in American history. It is an insightful, uniquely personal journey of fortitude, faith and resilience told by the young woman who stood alone and forced both the institution and the armed forces to look in the mirror. Janie Mines is one of the strongest women I know. Her story will stir the conscience of the reader and provoke a truly deeper conversation of race and gender relations in our country. Sadly, it reveals how culture can undermine and corrode the best intentions of law, policy, guidance, and the leadership.

—Patrick Walsh, graduate,
U.S. Naval Academy, Class of 1977

Janie Mines has taken the extraordinary effort to describe her life journey in service to her country. She takes you on her journey as a pioneer who persevered in faith through some challenging obstacles while keeping focused on her goals. This is a story about faith, about endurance, about dedication, about commitment and about taking advantage of opportunity. A wonderful life story instructive to many generations.

—Cecil Haney, graduate,
U.S. Naval Academy, Class of 1978

Janie's message of obedience, preparation, and faith resounds throughout this book. She overcame adversity to become the warrior leader we all desire in our Naval Academy graduates. As a former Superintendent of the U.S. Naval Academy who was an upperclass midshipman during her first two years there, I find her story disheartening for what she faced but inspiring for what she achieved.

—Jeffrey L Fowler, graduate,
U.S. Naval Academy, Class of 1978

A searingly honest personal narrative about her Naval Academy experience put in the context of the lessons learned in her childhood. Her tremendous respect for the institution and the Navy is clear, and her focus is on the wisdom and strength gained through adversity. I am very proud of my friend and classmate!

—Sandy Daniels, graduate,
U.S. Naval Academy, Class of 1980

Janie Mines has lived an amazing life, rife with challenges since her days growing up in Aiken, South Carolina to her emotional and historic journey as the first black female graduate of the United States Naval Academy. Throughout it all she has been true to her faith with the knowledge that God has a plan for her that presents itself in unique ways that show her true measure as a person and a leader. It's an honor to call her my friend and classmate.

—Reginald Trass, graduate,
U.S. Naval Academy, Class of 1980

I have known Janie Mines since the first days at the United States Naval Academy and have been blessed to have her as a dear friend for over four decades. It is a great honor for me to be able to share that with you here. Janie demonstrates her faith in God every day in every way, not in talk but in what she does and how she handles life's challenges. which have not been trivial. Having had a front row seat into the life of Janie, she has been a constant source of strength and help to me. She has shown me God's love and shared God's wisdom patiently, helping me to learn—and re-learn more than a few times—the peace of acceptance and the recognition that God has a plan for me too. Knowing that she is sharing her story with all of you brings me great joy. Becoming friends with Janie from the first days at the Naval Academy was not a coincidence—it was a gift. A gift that I am eternally thankful for!

—Janice L. Buxbaum, graduate,
U.S. Naval Academy, Class of 1980

I have known the author almost all of her life and she never ceases to amaze. And, this is no exception ... *No Coincidences*. Order my steps in thy word (as a child): and let not any iniquity have dominion over me (at the Academy), (paraphrasing Psalm 119:133). Insightful and inspiring reflections, this book is captivating from beginning to end. Well done.

—Gwendolyn Mines Boddie, graduate,
U.S. Naval Academy, Class of 1981

I have known Janie Mines for decades, and from our first encounter she has been a mentor and friend to generations. As an

African American graduate of the U.S. Naval Academy, I can attest that this is the book we have all been waiting for. I am inspired by her faith, leadership, selfless sacrifice, and generosity to others. I know that you will be as well.

—Natasha Sistrunk Robinson, graduate,
U.S. Naval Academy, Class of 2002

It was "No Coincidence" that the woman I sat next to my plebe year in Alumni auditorium for the mandatory basketball game I had been dreading attending was Ms. Janie Mines, the first black female graduate of the United States Naval Academy. I admired her and had seen her picture almost every day the year prior on a poster I had taped to my desk at NAPS. I couldn't believe I was meeting her. She welcomed me with open arms and spoke to me with such love and humility. She has been an angel and a source of strength for so many, especially midshipmen. She always taught us to think outside of ourselves and to try to understand the larger lesson. Thank you so much, Ms. Janie, for being there and pouring into us; I am so glad you are sharing your story.

—Shuntiyea Langston, graduate,
U.S. Naval Academy, Class of 2016

Throughout my years, Ms. Janie has been a wonderful mentor. Her kindness, ability to listen closely, and willingness to share wisdom and her experiences are all qualities I admire and to this day continue to learn from. She always strives to help me continuously better myself, and our regular conversations have helped me grow immensely, both personally and professionally. Beyond that, her support is a constant motivator, reminding me that I can accomplish anything I work hard for. Ms. Janie will always be a part of my life as a mentor, motivator, and mother figure.

—Deja Baker,
U.S. Naval Academy, Class of 2018

Janie Mines is a strong servant leader, master mentor, and ultimate teammate. Her sage counsel is sought and respected by juniors and seniors alike across racial, cultural, and economic lines. Her genuine love for America and its people is evident in all that she lives, breathes, and thinks. I can hardly wait to purchase *No Coincidences* for my leadership team, and it will be my Christmas gift for everyone I exchange presents with this upcoming Holy season.

—Evelyn "Vonn" Banks,
30-year Navy Veteran and Motivational Speaker

Contents

Foreword	x
Preface	xv
The Academy	xv
Why I Wrote the Book	xvii
What to Expect	xix
My Perspective	xx
Acknowledgements	xxi
Reflections	1
1 – I Don't Need You	3
2 – My Invisible Friends	14
3 – I'm Gonna Tell My Daddy	23
4 – Shock and Awe	37
5 – Collateral Damage	46
6 – Preparation for the Future	52
7 – I Don't Care What They Think	62
8 – Angels	73
9 – Contagion	83
10 – "What Did You Expect When You Came Here?"	92
11 – Use What You Have	103
12 – Silent Majority	111

13 – "What Is Your Objective?"	117
14 – Hold Your Tongue	125
15 – Through the Pain	134
16 – A Few Good Friends	145
17 – "When People Show You Who They Are…"	154
18 – Warrior Up	164
19 – What Not to Do	177
20 – Motivation	183
21 – Trust, Then Verify	192
22 – Heroes	203
23 – Fair	212
24 – "And This Too Shall Pass"	222
25 – What's Mine Is Mine	228
Closing	236
Addendum – USNA Organizational Structure	240

Foreword

In 1980, as a new junior officer stationed at the Naval Training Center in Orlando, Florida, I looked around and didn't see any officers, male or female, who looked like me. The U.S. Navy officer corps was only a little over 3% black, and only a fraction of that number were black females. Coming from a large, northeastern city where I could "see myself" in practically every profession, I didn't see any black female officers in my command—or on the entire base for that matter. I was in culture shock. As I contemplated my new naval commission, I asked myself, *What have I done? Did I really just join the Navy? What am I doing here?* Questions ran rampantly through my mind. Then I met Janie.

Janie and I were stationed at different commands on the same base, but our paths crossed, and we became fast friends. We met outside the Bachelor Officer Quarters (BOQ), which would be our residences for a short period of time on the base. There was nothing particularly special about the residences, but I do recall they didn't lend themselves to meeting people apart from those living in one's own building. As I learned my way around, walking in between the worn buildings, I ran into Janie. I often read about recent military history, and I found the new doors opening for women especially interesting. I knew who Janie Mines was, and I understood the historical significance of her journey to becoming a naval officer as the first black female graduate of the U.S. Naval Academy in Annapolis, Maryland. She had no idea who I was, and that was fine with me.

Janie Mines was genuinely happy. She readily engaged me in conversation and was curious about how I came to Orlando—and she laughed all the time. Surely, she had experienced extreme pressure to perform—*excel*—while attending the Naval Academy, but she was confident without arrogance, self-assured without judgment. The pressure she felt had to be greater than whatever I was experiencing as a newly commissioned officer at my command. She managed to graduate from Annapolis, and she remained confident, happy, and joyous. Even her photo in her Lucky Bag yearbook showed her sitting on a hot red Corvette expressing pure joy. *What had she endured?* I wondered. She showed up to the Naval Academy as the only black female in the entire brigade, she made it through four years of who knows what, and she obviously thrived to graduation and beyond. *But how?* I was even more amazed she didn't display any scorn or distain for others, given what she certainly must have been through. *How was that possible?* The many answers to those questions lay in her spiritual foundation, upbringing, and stamina, which she so graciously has chosen to share in *No Coincidences*.

Did I say stamina? Yes, I have to mention Janie worked out *constantly*. She took me along with her on 10- to 12-mile bicycle rides after a full day of work, jogs around the base, and swimming whenever she could fit it in. Physical fitness was a mainstay of her personal regimen. I discovered her fitness level helped her to endure whatever was thrown her way. She must have wanted to leave me in the dust a few times, but she never did. That's Janie.

You see, our meeting was no coincidence. Four years prior to our chance meeting at the BOQ in Orlando, I met Janie Mines for the very first time at a party after the 1976 Army-Navy football game. I recognized Janie as the first and only black female member of the first class of women to be admitted to the U.S. Naval Academy—just five months before. I knew this because for a very brief moment, I considered joining that same class. But I decided against it. I followed her admittance in the news with curiosity—and with some amount of envy. I remained curious, knowing she was there by herself. So, I approached Janie at the party. I introduced myself, told her I was proud of her, and asked how she was doing. She simply looked at me with no expression and said very little. I attributed her lack of response to perhaps she was shy—or understandably cautious. When I ran into her again in 1980, there was no shyness, no hesitation to talk, to trade jabs, or to work to physical exhaustion. This is the true Janie Mines.

Being stationed together in Orlando was the start of a very strong friendship which later became a family connection. Throughout the years, Janie shared several reflections of her time at the Naval Academy, and those reflections—among others—are contained herein. As I learned more about Janie, I marveled how her background made her uniquely qualified to attend the Naval Academy and to serve as a naval officer. She so aptly describes her background and spiritual foundation in this book of reflections. I saw—and often experienced—her incredible spiritual foundation through the years. I like to describe Janie's ability to persevere as the personification of three characteristics of her life: obedience to the Lord, ordered steps, and ordained to minister to and help others using her God-given talents.

Let me explain what I mean, first as introspective questions, then as definitive statements. One cannot help but to sometimes compare their own personal circumstances, reactions, and thoughts to others whom they meet—whether in-person, through a book, or on television. We ask ourselves, "What would I do? Would I be prepared to deal with a similar situation? Could I have tolerated this event until I figured out what was happening and what path to take to rectify the situation? Could I determine the motives behind someone else's actions? Would I lose my religion and fall back on street instincts?" When I contemplate all of the previous questions in the context of being the first black female to enter the Naval Academy, I determine I would have been ill-prepared to enter the Academy—let alone persist, graduate, and thrive still in my right mind. *But to what end?* I think I know to what end, and you will know, too, as a result of reading this book.

What I have learned about Janie over these many years is, first and foremost, she is obedient to God's Word. I'm not saying she's perfect and without blemish, but rather I'm speaking to the fact that she listens and hears God call. She then wrestles with His requests—like many of us do. But in the end, she will obey and follow the direction to the best of her ability, which is better than good.

Second, Janie's steps are ordered. I think what gives her a fearlessness regarding her life choices is her confidence God is ordering her steps. She acts knowing—*knowing*—God has her back, and there is nothing that can hold her back after that. This book is about preparation. After Janie prepared—even when she didn't know what she was preparing for—she stepped out on faith and it later became clear why she went through what she did.

Third, (and as the daughter of a pastor, Janie will dispute my characterization that anything about her is ordained), she is ordained to help and assist others, and to speak for others when they don't know what words to say. Her ability to accomplish the tough jobs with dignity and grace speaks to her previous two character traits—obedience and ordered steps; but her success in the face of forces and obstacles—many deliberately placed—is nothing short of supernaturally ordained. I have seen all three of these characteristics embodied time and time again.

Janie Mines helped me and others navigate our naval careers, first by understanding Navy culture. Her mentoring, however, went well beyond naval terminology and history, rules of the road for ships, and how to correctly wear our uniforms. Her mentoring was much more personal and sometimes felt like invasion of privacy as it was not always obvious why we were receiving certain counsel or what the outcome would be. Nevertheless, Janie has helped me and countless others grow personally, professionally, and spiritually—and, yes, the advice she so unselfishly provided was both accurate and timely.

It was by watching Janie that I discovered her faith got her through and allowed her to maintain her joy. This book, *No Coincidences*, will give you insight into her journey, her preparation, as well as what she learned about herself, and is certain to be of invaluable assistance to you, the reader, in your own personal journey. Enjoy Janie's reflections as they provide background, purpose, and spiritual reliance upon the Lord. I concluded many years ago—and you will understand clearly after you read this book—God sent the right one.

Laura Stubbs, Ph.D.
Captain, U.S. Navy, Reserve (Retired)

Preface

The Academy

The United States Naval Academy—affectionately referred to as "the Academy"—in 1976, as I saw it, was in some ways a very different place than it is now. The concept of retention was not a part of our vocabulary. Literally, we were told on the first day, "Look to you left and look to your right. One of you will not be here at the end." It was about identifying the weaknesses in individuals and forcing them to overcome them—or forcing them out the door.

So, how was weakness defined? The mission of the Academy was "To prepare Midshipmen morally, mentally, and physically to be professional officers in the naval service." From my observations, the most critical traits were honor, courage, composure under stress, physical bearing, endurance, and intellect—though not necessarily in that order. These traits seemed to be the foundation for a successful midshipman and naval officer. Anyone who didn't possess—or was incapable of attaining—these traits was deemed undesirable and unqualified to be a leader in the Fleet or Marine Corps. The implied goal was to identify these individuals and weed them out, strongly encouraging a different career choice—and, inherently, a different school.

To the naval service and the midshipmen, it was a matter of life and death. The Academy had to produce exceptionally honorable, resilient, and intellectual combat leaders able to successfully command under the most strenuous conditions imaginable. In this line of work, failure was not an inconvenience—it was a catastrophe. And therefore, *not* an option.

In 1976, black men affiliated with the military had only recently moved beyond the roles of cooks and stewards. Very few black men had graduated from the Academy, and some in the Navy still questioned their ability to successfully lead in a predominately white male Navy and Marine Corps.

Into this environment of 4,400 men, 81 women were inserted—and I was the only black one. No laws had changed to allow women to serve in combat. It was assumed by many that the Academy of 1976 would chew us up and spit us out. Some believed we were the very embodiment of the undesirable and unqualified leader who must never reach the Fleet or the Corps. To them, we were there taking up valuable slots from potential combat officers. At the time, there was no plan regarding how to deploy us upon graduation. Add to this the color of my skin, and I was called a "double insult" who could not be permitted to "get good white men killed."

So, the undesirable behaviors and events I describe in this book were not based simply on gender and race. Not to say these were not factors for some; but for most, it was much more complicated than that. They believed women and minorities as leaders were a threat to good order and discipline, resulting in a naval service unfit to perform its mission. My only recourse was to prove I embodied the traits of a successful naval officer. Based on the cultural norms and institutionalized beliefs, their only recourse was to ensure I didn't graduate.

Why I Wrote This Book

I really did not want to write this book. So why did I do it? Have you ever felt like there is something you must do and no matter how much you try to avoid it, there will be no peace until it's done? This book is the result of that overwhelming pressure, punctuated by my promise to two dear mentors mentioned in the Acknowledgements section of this book.

Many people have asked me to tell my story. I have struggled for decades with how to do this in a useful manner that didn't focus on the sensational. Additionally, I was concerned my story might reflect poorly on the Academy, an institution for which I have the greatest respect. I discussed this concern with midshipmen and graduates alike, and they unanimously shared their desire that I be honest with them. So, my goal is to strike a balance between honesty—my truth—and respect for an outstanding institution.

I know some of my Academy brothers and sisters will not be pleased with my literally, "speaking out of school." After all, what happens in Bancroft Hall, stays in Bancroft Hall. But this book details a challenging episode in the long and storied history of the Academy. It describes some of the highest highs and lowest lows that occurred during a time of significant change, not only at the Academy, but across the nation. I believe we do not progress by burying these experiences, but by sharing and discussing them. "Those who do not learn from history are doomed to repeat it," paraphrases a quote from the Spanish American philosopher George Santayana. I totally agree; although we have made progress as a country, much remains to be done. We must share.

So, I know writing this was the right thing to do. But again, I just didn't want to do it. I am a very private person and I'm sharing a lot of me with you. But, this was necessary to deliver the message that nothing in my life was coincidental. This book shares my life experiences from childhood through the Academy, but my personal "*No Coincidences*" truth remains in place still today.

What to Expect

While reading this book, I hope you will feel as though I am talking to you and sharing confidences as though we are the only two people in the room. We will laugh together, cry together, and there may even be some thoughts of, "I can't believe she said that!" So, if you will—please—keep my secrets.

This book represents my personal reflections. I am not attempting to share some great truths or wisdom of the ages. The content reflects my experiences, as I remember them. These experiences are shared as individual occurrences and collages of persons and events to avoid the appearance of referencing any specific individuals, living or dead. I am sharing my thoughts, opinions, reactions, and feelings. This is not a documentary. It is my story about a brief—but impactful—period of my life.

The format of this book is intentionally consistent throughout. Each chapter begins with my experiences as a youth growing up in the rural south and the lessons I learned from those experiences. The chapter continues with relevant events that occurred as a midshipman at the Academy. The prevailing theme is, these early experiences and preparations instilled tenacity, and were the exact foundations required—good and bad—for success as the first black female to attend the Academy — *No Coincidences*.

My Perspective

My roots run deep in Christianity and you will experience that influence in this narrative. Having said that, I am no biblical scholar and sometimes my language may be a bit graphic. For this, I apologize in advance. That part of me—although considerably improved since my youth—remains a work in progress. But, since I'm sharing, I am giving you access to the real deal.

In addition to being a Christian work in progress, I am a Southerner. My writing style and colloquialisms reflect these roots. I will ramble, go in and out of character, make random comments, and generally defy the norms of good literature. For this I do not apologize—I am who I am. If that bothers you, please do not read this book. It was not meant for you.

In conclusion, this group of reflections details the battles waged between a 19-year-old black female and an outstanding institution steeped in tradition, as it struggled through monumental change. I challenge you, as the reader, to see beyond the sensation of each battle and observe through my reflections the beginning of a cultural evolution—an evolution continuing today in a Brigade of Midshipmen in which minorities and women may soon represent the majority of the student body.

Acknowledgements

In memory of Staff Sergeant *Naason Griffin*, U.S. Marine Corps (Retired).

I express my gratitude to the following:

Reverend *William L.* and *Daisy S. Mines*, the best parents a nontraditional little girl could ever hope for.

My beloved sister, *Gwendolyn Mines Boddie*, the second black female to receive a diploma from the U.S. Naval Academy, and my dear son, *William*.

To my dear friends, Dr. *Laura D. Stubbs* and Rear Admiral *Sandy L. Daniels*, who both contributed in their own way to the completion of this book. And to my lifelong confidants and classmates, Ms. *Janice Buxbaum* and Mr. *Reginald Trass*, to whom I am also eternally grateful.

And finally, as I mentioned in the preface, many people have asked me to write a book about my experiences at the Academy. I produced three false starts before beginning this text. Again, I really didn't want to do this. But, on a winter morning in 2017, I asked a question of a woman for whom I have the utmost respect. I said, "Mrs. Close, you have done so much for other people. Is there anything I can do for you?" She briefly paused, and, as would be expected of any gracious southern lady, said, "Nothing, just keep being you and doing what you're doing."

I was a little disappointed by the answer because I really was sincere in my desire to honor her in some manner. I really wanted to do something for her. So, when I noticed she was giving her answer further thought, I was very excited—until I heard her response. "Write a book," she said. *Where did that come from!?* She got me like no one else had ever been able to do. *What could I say?* I asked her, and she answered. Never in a thousand years would I have guessed this would have been her answer.

My heart sank as I looked at her and asked, "A book?" I was hoping I had misunderstood her. She said, "Yes, write a book." If she was specific about the topic of the book, I didn't hear it. I was too busy mentally shooting myself. I had been feeling convicted by God about writing a book about the Academy for some time. I promised God on numerous occasions I would write it soon. Well, thanks to Mrs. Close, I would be writing that book right away. Although I am convinced she will probably outlive me, when you make a promise to your 90-plus-year-old mentor, there is an inherent sense of urgency.

Although she is going to hate this part, I feel compelled to tell you a little about this outstanding woman. She is a humble servant-leader who is reluctant to be visible. She prefers to work behind the scenes and let others be in the public eye. So, with her indulgence, the following helps to explain why she is so beloved.

Mrs. *Anne Springs Close*, born in 1925, is the only surviving child of Elliott Springs, a legendary flyer in World War I and an outstandingly successful businessman who made Springs Fabrics a household name. She graduated from schools in Fort Mill and Charleston, South Carolina before attending Smith College in Massachusetts.

As chair of the board of both the Springs Close Foundation, Inc. and Leroy Springs and Company, Inc., Mrs. Close expanded the efforts begun by her father. Since it was chartered, the Springs Close Foundation has contributed millions of dollars to projects designed to improve the quality of life and well-being for people in these communities. A perpetual contribution is the 2,300-acre Anne Springs Close Greenway for which Mrs. Close received the Pugsley Medal in 2001.

In that same year, Mrs. Close assisted me in my efforts to assist socioeconomically disadvantaged middle and high school boys. To this day she continues to be a blessing to the communities of Fort Mill, Chester, Lancaster, Rock Hill and the surrounding South Carolina communities. The fact Mrs. Close became a part of my life and answered my question in that manner was — *No Coincidence*.

Another key inspiration for the writing of this book was retired naval officer Lieutenant Commander *Wesley Brown* (April 3, 1927 – May 22, 2012). He was the sixth African American to attend—and the first to graduate from—the U.S. Naval Academy. Nominated for admission and later appointed to the U.S. Naval Academy by New York Congressman Adam Clayton Powell, Jr., LCDR Brown entered the Academy on June 30, 1945, graduating on June 3, 1949. He was an accomplished athlete, running cross-country with Jimmy Carter, the 39th president, who was also a Naval Academy graduate. LCDR Brown served in both the Korean and Vietnam Wars, and his naval service spanned from May 2, 1944 until June 30, 1969.

In addition to being an outstanding role model—embodying the traits of honor, courage, commitment, uncommon resilience, and tenacity—he was a consummate gentleman. Although I desired to meet him much earlier, I finally met him late in his life. I kicked myself for not more aggressively pursuing the opportunity to meet him earlier. When we met, he told me he had wanted to meet me for a long time. I was surprised and honored by this revelation.
I visited LCDR Brown several times and he listened with incredulity as I shared my experiences at the Academy. He, too, encouraged me to write a book. He joined the chorus in reminding me it was not

about me, but a story that needed to be shared. I still don't quite understand this sentiment, but I acquiesced. I promised to write a book, but unfortunately, I didn't fulfill this promise before he passed.

To Mrs. Close and Lieutenant Commander Brown, I express my undying gratitude for your encouragement and mentorship. For all you have done and all you represent, I dedicate this book to you.

Reflections

This is a book of "Reflections." I guess I should start by defining the term. In *Reflective Method of Philosophy*, Dr. Desh Raj Sirswal describes reflection as "an important human activity in which people recapture their experience, think about it, mull over, and evaluate it." Merriam-Webster defines a reflection more simply as "consideration of some subject matter, idea, or purpose." Both descriptions capture what I attempt to communicate in this book.

The reflections in this book represent a compilation of experiences, observations, and learnings which resulted in my perspective regarding topics that were critical to my survival. The reflection topics are also highly influenced by discussions with midshipmen over the years. As they shared their own challenges, inevitably we discussed options within the context of my experiences. On many occasions, I was asked to write down what I shared—or to repeat it—so the particular midshipman or young junior officer could write it down.

That response always surprised me. I never considered my responses to be deep philosophical thoughts worthy of noting. Although I did quietly pray before responding to each topic, and then I recommended the individuals pray and do what they felt was right for them. I did the same thing as I wrote each reflection in this book. And, I encourage you to be prayerful over all aspects of your life and move forward as you feel led.

In my final acquiescence to writing down these concepts, I struggled with the format. I *decided to* share my experiences in a format that communicates my personal learnings—my own reflections. Although discussed separately—and in no particular order—these reflections manifest as an interwoven quilt. The repetitions of certain aspects of my life are apparent; however, I share from the perspective of the particular reflection being discussed. As I think is true in most lives, truly impactful events, occurrences, or periods have a multifaceted influence on who we become.

So, fasten your seatbelts, place your trays in the upright and locked position, sit back, and relax as I share my personal thoughts and conclusions about how my youth prepared me for the Academy. There will be ups, downs, curves—and cliffs—but, *No Coincidences*. Join me on this journey of introspection. Hopefully, we both will benefit from the trip.

1 – I Don't Need You

In writing this reflection, I found out something new. I thought my emotional independence was viewed by the psychological world as a bad thing. You know, the old "no man is an island" and "a society must be codependent to thrive" ideologies. Don't misunderstand. I was—and remain—"all in" for being a value-added member of society. I just had absolutely no delusions our society welcomed me with open arms. In reading about this independent behavior to which I adhered, I found some psychologists believe this to be a strength. I guess it all boils down to two words: it depends. I hope these revelations continue to happen throughout the writing of this book. I enjoy learning.

As a child, independence didn't mean I didn't value approval from others, (although this is a related concept you will witness in other reflections.) It simply meant I seldom came to anyone else for anything that was truly important. If I couldn't figure out how to do it myself, then I was not trying hard enough. I might involve others in discovering the solution, but only acted as I personally felt led. It also meant I wouldn't give up when I faced difficulties. Quitting seldom crossed my mind. I lived for the challenge.

So, how and when did I become this way? It probably started when I was very young. Trying to psychoanalyze yourself over 55 years later—without a single, qualifying medical credential—is an interesting thing to do. But that's who I am. I do things like that. I just look for the logic. The

I Don't Need You

foundation of my "I don't need you" attitude was the result of an early life experience.

I was told my parents thought my mother was incapable of bearing children. Although she was very beautiful, she was afflicted with a physical disability affecting her ability to walk normally, as well as compromising her cardiovascular system. As a child, it was diagnosed my mother would not survive beyond her thirties. My father—who was older—lost a wife and baby in childbirth, and didn't want to experience that again. So, I believe I was a surprise (S-U-R-PRISE!).

Additionally, I came into my mother's life at a very difficult time. She worked as a teacher in Newberry, South Carolina—60 miles away from our home—and she boarded there. The family home was in Aiken, South Carolina. I was with family caregivers most of the time, which I believe significantly affected what we now describe as maternal bonding. To add to this difficult situation, my maternal grandmother was diagnosed with terminal cancer soon after my birth. So, my mother spent much of her time caring for my grandmother and working to help support the family.

In the middle of all this—ten months after I was born—my mother became pregnant with my sister, my only biological sibling. At this point, I think my parents had to know where babies came from, and were willing to have another child so I wouldn't grow up as an only child. This is just my conjecture. Maybe they thought the miracle couldn't happen twice. If so, double surprise!

I Don't Need You

My mother had so much going on that she didn't care for herself during her pregnancy, and my sister was chronically ill—"sickly" as we called it—when she was born. Doctors thought she would be lucky to survive. As would be expected, I was not the priority. The parent I spent most of my time with was my father. As a pastor and a self-employed groundskeeper for large estates in the area, he was quite busy. He was a master of horticulture. I spent so much time with my father, I was nicknamed "Billie" because his name was William. I acquired many of my traits from him. I believe this contributed to the initial foundation of my self-sufficiency, but there was a pivotal event I remember as a small child that sealed the deal.

I was raised in a white, cinder block home down a dirt road on a beautifully manicured lot. There was a huge magnolia tree in the front yard that bloomed with large white flowers. I loved that tree. It was great for climbing. Around the front porch were azaleas and roses and other beautiful plants I can no longer remember. There was a large front porch trimmed in red brick with wooden rocking chairs and a large bench swing. This was one of my favorite spots as a child.

Just inside the front door was the "forbidden zone." As many people from my era will remember, there were certain rooms designated for "company,"—our special guests. In our home, this included a formal open concept (before the architectural idea was popular) living room and dining room, as well as a guest bedroom. There was a beautiful, antique mahogany dining set in the dining room. In the

I Don't Need You

living room, there was a large floral sofa, four coordinated arm chairs, a coffee table, and end tables. They all sat properly on the ugliest, thick gold-and-brown shag carpet you've ever seen in your life. Two of the chairs bordered a brick fireplace, only ignited during the Thanksgiving and Christmas holidays. Except during these occasions—and when we had company—no one *ever* used these rooms.

It was in this living room the pivotal event I mentioned actually occurred. One day, I was searching for my mother in the house. I was about four years old and my sister was two. For some unknown reason, my mother was alone—sitting in the "forbidden zone"—in the green armchair to the right of the fireplace. She was staring out the open front door through the green hedged arch at the large vegetable garden which my father maintained on our two-acre city lot. This garden was just beyond the small front yard on the other side of the private dirt road. I wondered why she was there and what she was doing, but more importantly, I couldn't believe my luck. I never had the opportunity to have her undivided attention.

Without saying a word, I immediately approached her and climbed onto her lap. My mother was a slim, light-skinned woman, but she had ample breasts, and I nuzzled my head into them and just relaxed. I was totally quiet. I was in heaven, and I was terrified something would happen to disturb this magical moment. Unfortunately, I was right. My little sister toddled in and started crying, demanding I get down so she could sit on my mother's lap, which was where she spent most of her time. Remember, she was sickly. I didn't climb down but clung more tightly to my mother. I just wanted to have this one moment. I wanted it to be about me, just this once.

I will never forget my mother's response. "Now, Billie, get down and let your sister up. You know she's the baby, and she's sickly." I just raised my head and looked at her. I don't believe she saw the pain in my eyes. She was looking at my sister, who was standing right in front of her and throwing a fit. I quietly climbed down with tears in my eyes and walked away. I promised myself I would never let anyone make me feel that way again. I never climbed in her lap or sought affection from her again. My heart was broken.
Contrary to my four-year-old declaration, I did experience a hurt akin to that pain only one other time in my life—but that is entirely another story. There were times when "I wanted my Mama" later in life, but never to the extent I would be decimated if it didn't happen. I was determined to take care of myself.

Of course, as a child I couldn't take care of certain needs. My parents provided for us well, with food, shelter, clothing, and most of what we wanted. My father would try to give me extra attention, but I saw this as sympathy, and I didn't want anyone feeling sorry for me. Again, I didn't come to them for anything that was important to me. I got much of my instructions from my father's sermons and watching the way they lived. Although it wasn't perfect, it was mostly good. I learned from the imperfections as well. My parents espoused education was the key to independence, and I ferociously pursued knowledge. I was determined to be emotionally, physically, and financially independent. You can't imagine how important this trait was to my survival at the Academy — *No Coincidences*.

Having left my home just after the Fourth of July in 1976, I was not prepared for the majestic Academy campus. The Academy was an idyllic physical environment with a mixture of beautiful old buildings and relatively new ones, tree-lined walkways with artfully manicured bushes and flowers. Monuments and retired weapons of all sorts peppered the landscape. When I first saw it, I thought it was absolutely beautiful and was excited to join its ranks. I actually had no idea how unwelcome I was—and how critical my trait of independence would be to successfully navigate these treacherous waters.

There are so many examples of how my independence saved me at the Academy, it's difficult to choose one. One thing I had going for me was we were punished for "bilging"—or, not supporting—our classmates. At least publicly, my classmates in my company were not antagonistic. An interesting side effect that occurred as a result of growing up with an independent spirit: I didn't notice whether people were supporting me or not. I simply did not care. I was in "La-La Land" when it came to the opinions of others about me. My tendency to need very little support from other people proved to be a true blessing, especially in the classroom.

Academy professors and instructors have a light course load by design, so there is adequate time to provide "EI"—Extra

I Don't Need You

Instruction—for individual midshipmen. I was told it was a requirement to assist midshipmen who requested EI. I learned early on this didn't always include me.

I was blessed to have completed several college level classes as well as NJROTC—Navy Junior Reserve Officer Training Corps—in high school. I was fortunate a lot of the material wasn't totally foreign to me. The challenge for me was the difference in teaching style, and the standard formats required for providing information on tests to be counted as correct. It was not sufficient to come up with the right answer; it had to be regurgitated exactly as provided.

It can actually be more difficult to re-learn a concept versus being introduced to it for the first time. Even though my answers were correct, my grades didn't reflect it because I didn't deliver the answer precisely as prescribed. One instructor even informally accused me of cheating. He didn't believe I could have developed these alternative approaches on my own. But then, who could I be cheating with, if no one else completed the tests as I did?

So, *silly me*, I requested EI. It was reluctantly scheduled by the instructor. Why do I say, reluctantly? Because when I requested EI to better understand how he wanted to see my results documented, he stared down at me like I was a maggot, exhaled loudly, and said, "If we must!" We agreed on a date and time, and I cautiously hoped after this instruction period I would better understand how he wanted me to present my correct answers. I also naively desired to build a productive rapport—since he controlled my grade.

I Don't Need You

Based on the reception I received from almost everyone else and previous experience with this ~~jerk~~ instructor, my expectations were low. I fought back this negative gloom-and-doom attitude and was determined to make the best of this encounter. Whenever personal negativity started to rear its ugly head, I always told myself, "Satan, I rebuke you in the name of Jesus." My father taught me that, and it works.

On the agreed upon date and time, I left my room in Bancroft Hall—or simply "the Hall," the largest single dormitory in the United States, maybe the world—and walked through Tecumseh Court, pass the majestic eight-foot statue of the Native American Chief, and proceeded down the tree-lined brick walkway known as Stribling Walk. I continued on to the entryway of the building, passing other midshipmen as they went to and from their academic instruction. As usual, most people didn't even look at one another. (Except the black midshipmen; they usually acknowledged one another.) Most people were lost in their own survival pursuits. But, I liked it that way because the vast majority of the time when I did capture the attention of another midshipman, it would not bode well for me.

I climbed the stairs to the floor where the instructors' offices were and came through the door. Having never been on death row and experienced that final walk to execution, I cannot accurately say this is how I felt, but I dreaded every step that brought me closer to him. The door was closed so I knocked, identified myself, and requested permission to enter. He grumbled something—which I assumed was

10

I Don't Need You

permission—and I came through the door.

Oh, my goodness! It looked like a category five hurricane had struck, tossing the contents of the office from desk, to table, to chair. Even the floor was not spared the onslaught of paper and books and binders and folders, open, closed, new and old. I was later informed instructors' or professors' offices in this condition were actually badges of honor, displayed as a tribute to research prowess. I don't know, but it just looked like a disorganized mess created by an absent-minded curmudgeon. Any great scientific, technical, or philosophical epiphany resulting from that chaos would be viewed with a healthy dose of skepticism from me.

Anyway, I made the short journey past the obstacle course to stand before his desk. He was sitting in his chair and gazing intently at a piece of paper he held in his hand. Without even looking up, he gruffly asked, "Why are you here?" I thought he knew, but I gave him the benefit of the doubt. I thought maybe he had a lot of students and it was difficult to remember all the conversations. I didn't realize this was just the opening comment to an extended assault regarding how stupid he believed me to be. I was told everyone else knew the material, so why didn't I? He asked why I was wasting his time, and stated if I couldn't keep up, I should just leave.

All I heard was *yada, yada, yada*! My conscious mind left the room as an act of self-preservation. I had violent tendencies—which was not altogether a bad thing in a school for warriors—but they had to be controlled. In order

I Don't Need You

to do this, my violently predisposed conscious mind would act out exploits in a fantasy world in which all parties would survive, but with differing levels of health. Because, in this particular fantasy, my fist shot out so forcefully, driving that piece of paper so far down his throat, that it acted as a dry colonic before I pulled it back through his body and used the residue from the journey to wipe that shit-eating grin off his face. Instead, I performed my silent, "Satan, I rebuke you in the name of Jesus" ritual. I tried to explain that I did know the material, but he could only accept one approach to an obviously multifaceted problem.

Uuugghhh! What did I say that for? He blew his top! He felt I was calling him stupid and became very defensive. He began yelling at me for accusing him of not understanding the material well enough to be able to follow alternative problem-solving methods. That actually didn't cross my mind until he said it. His anger in expressing himself, regarding this perceived attack on his intelligence, reminded me of a line in Shakespeare's play *Hamlet*: I believed he "doth protest too much."

I could hear movement in the halls as others heard the tirade. This interrupted my second round of internal musing in which I saw him as a screaming infant desperately in need of breast feeding and a diaper change. I guess the amusing thought must have shown on my face because he then asked me what the hell I was smiling at. My response was, "I'll find out, sir?" This was one of the five acceptable responses a "plebe"—college freshman—was to provide when questioned by an authority figure. A puzzled look

I Don't Need You

came across his sweaty, plum-colored face as he digested my response. This was quickly replaced by inflamed anger as he correctly surmised my intent. He jumped up from his desk, pointed at the door, and yelled at me to "Get out!"

As I walked back down the long hall, I thought, *Oh, sista-gurl, you did it now!* I knew not only was I on my own but, if at all possible, it was going to go even further downhill from here. The constant degrading comments in class continued—meant to demoralize me and convince others I was uniquely stupid. I'm so glad they couldn't read my mind.

So, as you might imagine, I didn't receive EI from him or most of the other professors and instructors. I fell back on my independence skills and learned to capture material verbatim, paying close attention to any conscious or unconscious indicators from the instructor of what would actually be on tests. I focused my studies on those materials and did well. I still didn't get the grade I earned, but he couldn't fail me.

I learned quickly not to expect academic assistance from my professors or anyone else. I never requested EI again. Sometimes people helped anyway, but that was "gravy"—an unexpected luxury. Although a painful experience for a lonely little girl, I am so appreciative of the day my mother told me to get down from her lap — *No Coincidences.*

2 – My Invisible Friends

My Daddy was the typical loud, emotionally engaging Missionary Baptist minister. He could make sounds and random noises that were unintelligible but were all a part of his arsenal for getting his point across. Reverend William Loyd Mines taught me more from his pulpit than I realized at the time. One of his constant themes was the Holy Trinity—the Heavenly Father, Son, and Holy Spirit—my three Invisible Friends. He used several scriptures to pull it all together. This included:

> *1 John 5:* [5] *Who is he that overcometh the world, but he that believeth that Jesus is the Son of God?* [6] *This is he that came by water and blood, even Jesus Christ; not by water only, but by water and blood. And it is the Spirit that beareth witness, because the Spirit is truth.* [7] *For there are three that bear record in heaven, the Father, the Word, and the Holy Ghost: and these three are one.*

Now, my little girl's mind had a difficult time wrapping itself around this concept. My father basically explained it this way. God in heaven walked among man through his son on earth, Jesus. When his son died and returned to God, they left us with the Holy Ghost to always dwell in and among us. I could kind of get this explanation, but the most important thing to me was that between the three of them, they had everything covered and I had no worries—if I believed. That was my bottom line.

My Invisible Friends

Believing was not difficult because this was all I knew. My father pastored two churches, one in a small town about thirty minutes away called Johnston, and one near my hometown in Aiken County. It was not uncommon for pastors to have multiple churches in the rural south.

As a child, my family was either on the way to church, in church, leaving church, or visiting church people. There were few regular exceptions—most of them governmental involving school, work, or other activities required by "Caesar." In this world, God, Jesus, and the Holy Ghost were just a fact of life. Just like breathing, living, and dying. It never crossed my mind to question this.

The Johnston church was in a small town almost exclusively comprised of black and white people. In those days, there was very little multicultural diversity in this part of the country. When driving into town, we passed a small black church; very plain, small, individual homes; and an affordable housing area populated predominately by black people. Folks were friendly and greeted one another on the streets. There was an attractive medium-sized car dealership which seemed so out of place to me in this small town.

Just after we crossed the railroad tracks hung the only traffic light in town we saw on our way to church. The light was at the intersection with the main street through town. This area contained most of the commercial businesses. I think I even remember a five-and-dime store, a gas station, and my favorite grocery store, Piggly Wiggly, being in the area. I just loved that name: Piggly Wiggly. The mascot was a jovial pig on the outside of the store. (If he ever went inside and visited the meat counter, he would not be so happy. No part of the pig was spared in the South. But I digress...I do that a lot.)

We proceeded through a neat, well-manicured neighborhood of brick houses, a radio station, and a well-kept brick school. This was literally the other side of the tracks. On the outskirts of town was my father's church. It sat back from the road with a large area of green grass in the front, always neatly mowed. The structure was white and relatively large for a rural church. It even had indoor toilets, which was not always a given in rural South Carolina. Although outhouses were usually clean, they terrified me. But you do what you have to do when nature calls. On the second and fourth Sundays, we were in Johnston. On the first and third Sundays, we were in Aiken. Eventually, my father had just one church in Aiken County and this was where I received the Word, sang in the choir, and obtained regular spiritual guidance about my Invisible Friends.

I was thoroughly indoctrinated with the reality and power of these Invisible Friends of mine. Every minister I heard unanimously confirmed the consequences for disbelief, and I wanted no part of those consequences. It's interesting how nebulous concepts can be brought into clear perspective by a good example. We were coming home from my daddy's Johnston church and passed through the small town of Eureka. No lights, no stop signs, just passing through. Oh,

My Invisible Friends

my goodness! It was the hottest day I can remember, with what seemed like waves of heat radiating from the pavement. It was absolutely miserable and there was no escaping the heat that took my breath away. On the church sign as we passed through Eureka was the phrase, "Hell is even hotter than this!" Enough said. God didn't need to tell me twice. I never wanted to experience anything hotter than that day. My Invisible Friends were real!

The point is God, Jesus, and the Holy Ghost were very real to me, and I was absolutely sure of this fact. My experiences in my father's churches indelibly printed this resolution in my mind, but it was my unique relationship that chiseled it in my heart. This relationship was built in the mind of a small, lonely girl, desperately in need of a friend.

Since my younger sister's health was fragile when she was small, she seldom came outside. Although I was permitted to play outside, I couldn't leave the yard. Fortunately, the yard was an approximately two-acre wooded lot in a small neighborhood where the other homes sat adjacent to one another. I could sometimes see and hear other children playing, but I couldn't join them. So, God, Jesus, and the Holy Ghost became my best friends, my playmates, and my confidants. It was a real, tangible relationship. I spent most of the day talking to them.

We loved playing cowboys and Indians. Well, at least I did. My father told me one day he looked out from the bedroom window and saw his small daughter dragging an axe across the backyard, heading for the woods. He came running out and asked what I was doing. I told him I needed more trees to build my forts. He wanted to know why I needed more than one fort. I said God and I were the cowboys, and Jesus and the Holy Ghost were the Indians (sorry, I didn't know to say 'Native Americans' back then) and we needed separate forts. I told him Jesus' and the Holy Ghost's fort didn't have to be that good, "because they were gonna lose anyway." In my mind, even though they were as one, I still felt as if God had the upper hand. So, naturally, I always picked Him to be on my team. My father took the axe from me and knocked down a few more rotten trees to finish "our" forts. I never told anyone else who I was talking to in the woods. When I grew older, my sister and neighborhood kids would join me, so my Invisible Friends were less prominent in my playtime. But, I knew they were always nearby.

Every decision, teenage crisis, and challenge were discussed with this trio. When we were small, my sister and I said the Lord's Prayer every night. I always wondered why I needed to do this since I had been talking to them all day. But, this was the prayer Jesus instructed us to say so theoretically, it did put a nice ribbon on my day. I say theoretically, because we had not finished talking yet. In bed, before I went to sleep, we recapped every question and concern from the day and I asked them what I should do. Besides sleeping better, the other huge advantage was that I woke up with answers. The first time I heard someone say they should "sleep on it" before deciding how to address an issue, I thought, *But of course! Isn't that what everyone does?*

My Invisible Friends

Imagine taking this kind of power to the Academy. I could never be truly lonely. I had someone to take my problems to, and I always received wise counsel. Who could ask for more? My experience as a lonely child raised to seek a personal relationship with God was — *No Coincidence.*

My Invisible Friends were needed at the Academy, just like they were needed by the lonely little girl in South Carolina. They returned to the day to day forefront of my existence, because at the Academy, I was invisible to the vast majority of the Brigade of Midshipmen—the student body—as well as the professors, instructors, and officers. I think most assumed I wouldn't be there very long, so why bother to acknowledge me?

Some of the upperclass black midshipmen would invite me to church and let me hang out with their reluctant girlfriends after services. My black classmates and I were invited to join the Seventh Battalion. The Brigade was comprised of six regular battalions, but the black midshipmen referred to themselves as the Seventh Battalion—or 7th Batt—forming an unauthorized organization to provide mutual support and social engagement with others facing similar challenges. Although there was empathy, no one could truly understand or fill the void of being alone in that environment. But, I greatly appreciated both gestures of inclusion.

I received important social sustenance from my involvement with the 7th Batt, but not all black midshipmen were supportive. Some felt there were a limited number of leadership positions set aside for minorities, regardless of how many were qualified. Now that women were being added to the list of marginalized groups, some black males actually told me black female midshipmen would be used as a "two-fer"—a two-for-one double minority taking what few opportunities there were for black men.

Others felt it was their personal responsibility to ensure I didn't have it easier because I was a woman. These were the guys that really pissed me off! What idiots! On what planet did they think my experience as a black female in this environment would be easy? Fortunately, this group was small. And as they insulted my appearance and motivation, I just couldn't believe they were not only so very cruel, but monumentally ignorant.

And then there were some black male midshipmen who just didn't believe women belonged at the Academy at all, believing women couldn't lead men. Women had traditional roles throughout history and this group believed I should be fulfilling one of those socially acceptable roles. They believed women were inherently inferior. *Sound familiar?* Sometimes I wondered if they could hear themselves.

I didn't talk to my female classmates very much. I think most of them saw me as some oddity in their midst. They were too busy trying to survive their own circumstances to willingly align themselves with an obvious target for unpleasant attention. While most left me alone, there was one woman who I *thought* was okay. Our interests were very different, but I thought she was nice, and I did talk to her. I learned later she was deliberately misrepresenting everything I said, destroying any relationship I built with other women. I still wonder today if she got extra privileges for keeping me isolated from the other women.

There was one woman who I really liked. She was great, and I loved her as a dear friend. It was so nice having her in my life. I didn't realize how much I missed having a female friend in addition to my invisible ones. Then one day, she just stopped talking to me. I tried to find out what I had done. I could be a little rough around the edges—and rather blunt with my young adult know-it-all wisdom—so I thought maybe I had said something to offend her. She wouldn't discuss it, and we never talked much after that. I wonder to this day if the relationship-sabotaging female who I had in my life had gotten to her, too. If so, it's so disappointing my one friend allowed someone to destroy our relationship.

Most of the time, my early years at the Academy were void of meaningful social interactions, and I was very grateful to have my Invisible Friends. They were no longer standing on the periphery like they did when my sister and friends joined me in the forts I once only occupied with them. They were front and center again. I usually only talked to them when I could find a solitary space. People might have thought I had lost it. The four of us would venture to the catacombs or the Jewish Chapel, and I would tell them about my day, asking what I should do. I always felt better after our discussions.

My Invisible Friends

My seclusion was not all bad, and it proved to be a totally ineffective tool in the ongoing efforts to get me out. Being ignored by the Brigade was actually much better than the alternative. I was happy as a pig in slop when most of them didn't talk to me. If anything, it brought me even closer to my Invisible Friends. Now the four of us were on the same team, protecting the one fort. All of their power was at my disposal. We were indestructible — *No Coincidences*.

3 – I'm Gonna Tell My Daddy

Sometimes people can be just plain mean. Trying to understand would leave me in a total state of confusion. So, in my youth, I didn't try to understand why. I just reacted with a fury—leaving everyone observing my reaction totally stunned. This behavior was diametrically opposed to my character 99% of the time. I never started the negative situation, and I had little patience for playing it through. I just wanted it to end so I could continue with more productive activities. My theme was, "I would not start it, but would most decisively end it."

These interactions were usually instigated by someone seeking attention or the favor of their peers. I was a target because I was physically very thin, extremely well-mannered, well-dressed, academically gifted, and friendly with everyone. The verdict was that "I thought I was white." I found this statement very insulting. It was a shame a part of our national discourse covertly and consistently communicated messages reinforcing the belief only white people possessed these desirable traits.

I had several options for addressing these attacks. I could have reported it to my parents, teachers, and in some instances, law enforcement. More importantly, I could have turned it over to my Heavenly Father. But, I didn't. Of course, I told him about it, but I didn't turn it over to him to resolve. There's a big difference. My response was to aggressively address the situation based on the type of attack. If it was verbal, I gave the aggressor a tongue

I'm Gonna Tell My Daddy

lashing, leaving them totally humiliated and confused. Why confused? Because my vocabulary was exhaustive. Between some of the words—whose meanings were obvious to any simple moron—were terms the typical youth didn't experience.

This type of unpleasant encounter once occurred on the playground when a girl—whose much larger frame could be attributed to the fact she had probably failed at least two grades—approached me with her small posse and called me a skinny black bitch. The girl's head bobbed from side to side, and she pointed her finger at my face. She accused me of walking around like I thought I was some queen; and that I thought I was cute, but I "wasn't shit." She said I made her sick, and I had better stay out of her way or she would knock that smile off my face. I was totally shocked—but mildly amused. I had no idea who this girl was, beyond the fact she had a reputation as a bully. I had never spoken to her, but you couldn't miss her because she was so big.

Anger quickly replaced my state of shock. I glared up at her, calling her an addle-minded buffoon. I told her I was not the source of her being sick, but having to look in the mirror at that pock-marked, dirty, zit-filled face was probably the catalyst for her illness, and likely symptomatic of some sexually transmitted disease. (I really didn't know what that was, but I heard an older cousin talk about it, and it sounded really bad.) A crowd started to gather as it always did in these situations. People laughed, asked one another for definitions, and generally made fun of her. I stated rather loudly how I found it incredulously ironic someone as detestable as she, who obviously knew nothing about good looks, had the nerve to comment on someone else's appearance—especially since she was obviously a dirty, filthy piece of street trash with the face of an orangutan's ass. I ended my tirade with an apology to all orangutans everywhere. (There probably are a few expletives deleted here and there, but you get the gist.)

She just stared at me while the crowd laughed at her—telling her to put up or shut up. I was so angry, I hissed at her that if she touched me, she would know she had been in a fight for many years to come. I shouted to her my intent to use every weapon and dirty trick at my disposal to permanently scar and cripple her if I could. She was big, and I wasn't going to let her hurt me. Tears were in her eyes as she walked away. I, too, turned and left—still full of adrenaline and feeling rather proud of myself.

Several days later, I talked to my father and the subject of mean, bullying people came up. I proudly told him how I had handled the bully at school. There was an obvious look of disappointment on his face as he asked me why I had done that. I looked at him like he was crazy, asking what was I supposed to do? Let her talk to me any kind of way she wanted, and threaten me? Was I supposed to let her get away with that? What should I do? Run home and tell my daddy? They would be whipping my butt every day at school if I did that.

He responded that I should have told my "Heavenly Daddy" who is always there for me, and I should have answered her

I'm Gonna Tell My Daddy

with love. I again looked at him like he was insane. I said, "I will answer her with love, alright. Only if I have 'love' written on the bottom of my shoe when I stomp her in her face!"

He just looked at me and shook his head. He asked, "Why do you think she behaved the way she did? Does she have two good parents, like you do, to teach her right from wrong? Does she have someone to help her and guide her when she's troubled? Does she have enough food, clothing, and a nice comfortable home, so that she's not concerned about her basic survival? Is she as blessed as you?" I sat, while he continued. "Maybe instead of humiliating her," he said, "you should have told your Heavenly Daddy and asked him for the words of love to share with her." He cautioned she would probably never forget that day for the rest of her life, and her self-esteem—which was probably already low—might now be permanently scarred.

My juvenile mind was not trying to hear this. I asked him what I was supposed to do if she was not receptive. He explained most people are receptive to sincere acts of love. But in any case, if she continued the behavior, I was to take it to my Heavenly Daddy, and He would take care of it. "That takes too long!" I said. "I don't want some eventual resolution in Heaven. I need to stop this kind of attack now." My father said, "If you turn it over to Him, do nothing further but just show love to the person. His response is swift and certain. Remember, God said He would fight these battles for us and vengeance is His."

I'm Gonna Tell My Daddy

In the typical fashion of most youth, I heard my father, but acted like I thought he was clueless and completely out of touch with my generation. I did change my behavior toward her, and although I didn't apologize, I did speak to her and tried to be nice. I could tell she was surprised and appeared relieved by the change. We never became friends, but we were cordial acquaintances. This encounter troubled me all my life. I was no longer proud of it and was ashamed of myself. That act of vengeance likely left us both with permanent scars.

I was not sure this "Tell my Daddy" thing would work. As usual, this topic of taking our burdens to God and leaving them there was the subject of many of my father's future sermons. He always did this to reinforce his point to me while I was part of a captive audience. It was interesting growing up with my life being preached from the pulpit. But, he did plant the seed, and I really tried. I never spoke to another child the way I had to her. I understood the concept of "telling Daddy," but didn't understand its power until I employed it at the Academy. This was a lesson well learned — *No Coincidences*.

Vengeance was rarely my motivation at the Academy. It was deterrence. I was too busy ducking and dodging to worry about getting revenge. My reactions had to be swift and visible. I believed I must show overt courage and cunning so all would-be comers knew there would be consequences. I believed this is what God led me to do. Since vengeance was not the focus, I felt no lingering ill-will toward my aggressors. Although in the moment, I usually felt anger and probably expressed some unkind thoughts—usually about white people—it quickly dissipated. I got my emotions under control and returned to my logical state.

Telling Daddy was not reserved only for those who did damage for truly malicious reasons, but also for the misguided who believed they were doing the "right thing." Both groups could produce equally detrimental results. Although I encountered numerous situations, very few captured as much wide-spread interest—and did as much harm—as an article written by a well-respected 1968 graduate, "Women Can't Fight."

As Academy midshipmen, we looked up to our alumni, especially the war heroes who demonstrated everything we were learning in the most intense situations imaginable. Although many of these alumni were not supportive of women at the Academy—and only marginally accepting of blacks—few chose to publicly attack the institution and the brave women who broke the gender barrier.

In my senior year at the Academy, an alumnus totally decimated the almost four years of progress women had made. In November 1979, he wrote a scathing article in the *Washingtonian* magazine, well-summarized in the introduction:

> *"In this story, a Naval Academy graduate, a combat veteran of Vietnam, says the country's fighting mission is being*

> *corrupted, with grave consequences to the national defense. One of the main problems, he says, is women."*

The following are several quotes from that article:

> *"And I have never met a woman, including the dozens of female midshipmen I encountered during my recent semester as a professor at the Naval Academy, whom I would trust to provide those men with combat leadership."*

> *"Now you cannot physically punish a plebe. You cannot unduly harass a plebe. God forbid that you should use abusive language to a plebe."*

> *"The Hall, which houses 4,000 males and 300 females, is a horny woman's dream."*

> *"Courage comes in many forms. And today at the Naval Academy, courage sometimes means simply stating your opinion when it varies from prescribed policy. I'd much rather have been in the last class with balls than the first class with women."*

> *"A male and female were convicted of the same honor offense at the same time. The man was thrown out. The woman was put on*

probation."

"Males in the society feel stripped, symbolically and actually. I wonder if that doesn't tie into the increase in rapes over the past decade. Rape is a crime of revenge, not passion. In any event, the real question isn't the women. The real question is this: Where in this country can someone go to find out if he is a man? And where can someone who knows he is a man go to celebrate his masculinity? Is that important on a societal level? I think it is."

"What of the women themselves? There are now about 300 female midshipmen at the Naval Academy, surrounded by some 4,000 males. The women wear men's clothes, with slight variations. They live in a closed, pressurized environment where they are outnumbered almost fifteen to one by men, 24 hours a day. They are emerging into womanhood almost alone, in an isolation that resembles a tour of duty on a desert island. They study a man's profession, learn the deeds of men, accept men as role models. They seem spirited but confused, tolerated but never accepted. They are for the most part delightful women, trusting and ambitious and capable in many ways, and I admire them, more for who they are than for

> *what they are doing. As for what they are doing, it would be unfair not to mention that no other group of women in this country has ever undergone such a prolonged regimen, however watered down. But I cannot escape a feeling that even the women are losing, that someday they will come to believe they lost more than they gained inside those walls."*

And as a conclusion, commenting on a senior military officer's concern regarding gender-integrated training, the article stated:

> *"...He is the only combat veteran of World War II, Korea, and Vietnam now serving on the Joint Chiefs of Staff. He is one of the most decorated Marines in history, a campaigner who led guerrilla troops in central China, a rifle company during the Chosin Reservoir breakout in Korea, and an infantry regiment in Vietnam, where he was known as one of the few "fighting colonels."*

> *"I told this to a woman friend of mine, a law school classmate who is now an attorney in Washington and with whom I frequently discuss sexual roles. She was unimpressed with [his] credentials.*

I'm Gonna Tell My Daddy

"She wanted to know what he knew about women."

This single article turned the clock back almost four years.

"Oh my God, have you seen it?" asked a female classmate, a combination of rage and fear in her voice.

I had no idea what she was talking about. "Calm down. Seen what?" I asked. I knew it couldn't be that bad. Probably just an unflattering sheet poster or temporary wall graffiti disparaging women.

She almost yelled. "The article written by that asshole about women at the Academy. The guys are walking around shoving it in women's faces. It's being used to justify a renewed attack on women at the Academy."

First of all, she was going to have to be a lot more specific. "Which asshole?" I asked. "What article?"

She described what she read.

I was furious—and fearful, too. Things had finally calmed down. The first class of women was about to graduate. The plebe year that, according to the article, women didn't have was about to reignite. The plebe year—the most mentally and physically demanding freshman year—where some women were beaten, attacked by multiple men, spit on, cursed, academically cheated, constantly bombarded by threats, and generally unprotected by senior leaders—*that* plebe year. The plebe year we didn't have? How ignorant could one man be?

So, what does this have to do with telling my Daddy? Well, that's exactly what I did, but not until after I began to write a scathing book called, *A Sense of Humor*. It was to be a parody of a book written by this misguided graduate entitled, *A Sense of Honor*. As far as I was concerned, anyone who could write that article knew nothing about honor, and the many minions he had following him from across the Brigade deserved to be taken down a notch. And I, as detailed from my childhood experiences, was good at that.

So, I began to write a tell-all—in excruciating detail—about some weak, "wanna-be men," and what Academy women had endured at the hands of "America's finest." What would people think, when they read about the atrocities being visited upon women, whose only crime was choosing to serve their nation and die for it, if needed? I was going to bring this hell-hole to its knees. Women, who had spent the last four years accomplishing what few men could have endured? And this ~~simpleton~~ misguided young man had the nerve to infer we were there because it was a "horny woman's dream."

The fact this article would ~~whine about~~ comment on disparate treatment regarding an honor offense when women were attacked in manners warranting felony criminal charges—but were addressed with conduct demerits, if addressed at all. I was going to challenge what kind of "balls" it took to perform these crimes in an environment where your targets were outnumbered 4,400 to 81. What kind of "courage" was required to speak out in a climate that, generally, overtly and covertly celebrated this behavior and the words of this article. *Ooooh, such brave men!? Give me a break!* I was going to tell it all.

At least until I heard my father's words in the back of my mind asking, "Why did you do that?"

I remembered our discussion about how cruelly I attacked my juvenile aggressor. It made me question my motives and whether the book I was writing would make the environment better. Would the Academy really change, or would it close ranks to protect itself? Would the women be forced to choose between discrediting my book or loosing what they fought for during the past four years? Did I have the right to place women—so eager to be accepted and to change the attitudes of the Academy—in this situation? In writing the book, I would have publicly attacked the reputation of an institution for which we had fought to be a part. An institution, oddly enough, we had come to care about, willing to defend it from any threat. Did I have the right to heap more coals on an already all-consuming flame—all in the spirit of revenge?

I chose the alternative my father taught me. I told my "Daddy." Every night, I fell on my knees and asked God for this alumnus to be given exactly what he deserved. Even after I graduated, I remembered him in my prayers because women were still having that article shoved in their faces.

I'm Gonna Tell My Daddy

This alumnus continues to be representative of the standard bearer for hateful male behavior toward women at the Academy. When he received high ranking positions decades later, female graduates and current female midshipmen protested. (I was told women lined the trees of Stribling Walk with their underwear on just one such occasion.) Women have repeatedly gone to the media to share what his single-minded act of childish rebellion had done—and continued to do—to Academy women. And forty years later, when he was about to receive the highest award Academy graduates can bestow upon fellow graduates, women protested—and he did not participate in the awards ceremony.

What is sad is this: except for that article, he probably deserved the honor. I wonder how most of us would fare if we were judged almost forty years later by our written social network comments? As I look back on the situation, I realize it was written by a young man, not much older than my son is now. A young man, likely influenced by senior men he trusted and respected. A young man who cherished the Academy and only understood one type of combat and combat officer. A young man who did not see the dawn of the "Information Age," nor the need for highly qualified combat officers who would wage war in the cyber world. Because he had never experienced it, he could not imagine there were women who would fight tenaciously and intelligently to destroy *any* adversary threatening what she so deeply cared about. This alumnus would have done well to have heeded the last line of his article and applied it to himself: *"She wanted to know, what does he know about women."*

I am in no way justifying what this alumnus did. It still angers me. Not because of the words he wrote, but because of what happened to women as a result of these words. He achieved nothing but needless harm. And I almost did the same thing. But unlike this alumnus who failed to listen to his female attorney friend, I listened to the words of my Fathers, both earthly and heavenly. Now I pray for healing. I pray pride and revenge will waste away, and Academy brothers and sisters can learn from this experience. The fact that I learned to "Tell my Daddy" as a child was — *No Coincidence.*

4 – *Shock and Awe*

Ferocious and unrelenting attacks by superior forces, strong-arming adversaries to quickly concede defeat, were nothing new. This physical aggression designed to not only achieve conquest but to generate perpetual fear took it to another level. I think sometimes I brought this behavior out in people because I wouldn't give up. No matter how superior the force, they had better keep me down because if I thought I was doing the right thing, I was coming back.

As I was growing up, my parents would take care of cousins needing to—or wanting to—live with us. They were older and initially much larger. I still wouldn't tolerate attempts at physical dominance from them. One male cousin was like a big brother to me, and he allowed me to hang out with him. He was always trying to teach me about everything—from boys to martial arts—and was usually pretty mellow. On one occasion, he was in a particularly bad mood, likely from being disciplined for breaking a rule or not being allowed to do something he wanted to do. Our family's rules were particularly difficult for him, as he was an older teen accustomed to coming and going as he pleased. That was not happening in my parents' house. As long as you lived in their house, you followed their rules. He was uncharacteristically grumpy that day.

My parents weren't home and had left us there with him. As usual, our chores were expected to be done before they returned. My cousin reminded me—in a very loud and rude tone—I needed to get some cleaning done. Although he was five to six years older, (and I really looked up to him), I was not even mildly submissive. Typically, I would have responded with a, "Who in the hell do you think you're talking to?" but I realized he was in a bad mood. I decided to just ignore him. This *really* made him angry. He grabbed me and yelled, "Are you deaf?"

I admit, managing anger when attacked was not a strength. My cousin's attempt to shock me into submission blew up in his face, as he became the victim of a volley of kicks and punches from every conceivable angle. He was much bigger and stronger, but I didn't even care. My father told me no man was to touch me in any way that made me uncomfortable, and he left physical discipline to my mother. Since my father didn't put his hands on me that way, unequivocally, no one else would either!

At first, he just tried to block the blows, but he soon learned that although I was physically smaller, I was strong—and my blows hurt. Then he tried to grab me. I responded with projectiles. Anything I could get my hands on, I threw. Lamps, books, anything I could pick up. I tried hitting him with a broom handle, but when he took that from me, I resumed the aerial attack. He kept trying to tell me to stop. I wouldn't. I damaged windows, furniture, and flooring before he finally grabbed me, threw me down, and pinned my arms while sitting on my legs. This only served to make me angrier, and whenever a hand worked free, I grabbed one of the many items strewn on the floor and swung for his head. I kept yelling at him about putting his hands on me. My mother was the *only* person allowed to do this.

Shock and Awe

He started apologizing and begging me to stop. He stayed on top of me until exhaustion slowed my attacks, and I grudgingly accepted his apology. I told him the next time he put his hands on me, one of us was leaving this earth. We never fought again.

When my parents came home, they didn't spank me. I think they were in shock. I was about 5'5" and less than 90 pounds—all lace, bows, and pigtails. I told them what happened and reminded my father of his instructions. He just looked at me, still in shock. They didn't know I had that in me. Neither did I. My cousin explained what happened in more detail, but basically agreed with me regarding the provocation. My mother told us to clean up the mess, my father made repairs, and they both looked at me like I had two heads.

I always wanted to study martial arts, and my cousin recommended this to assist me in managing my anger when physically challenged. He knew some karate and practiced at home, showing me various self-defense techniques. I would try to mimic his moves and jumped at the opportunity to receive formal training, but my emotional volatility followed me to my new *dojo*.

When I visited the *dojo*, the first thing I noticed was how disciplined the training was. It was overseen by a very formal and disciplined middle-aged man, who I later describe as an angel. The actual instructors were two young black men, equally focused and disciplined.

Shock and Awe

The second thing I noticed was there were no females. This didn't bother me in the least. I was accustomed to being the only black and/or female in most settings outside of home and church. It just always seemed to be that way.

Naturally inquisitive, I asked a few questions: the style of karate, the trophies displayed, the schedule, the equipment, the promotion process, and the cost. The young black male instructor was very helpful. I liked what I heard, and I especially liked what I saw. Everything I saw. The instructors were really cute. It didn't take long to get over this infatuation.

I still didn't like to be physically challenged, but in a very short period, I learned the basics and progressed to controlled sparring. Then, unfortunately, I did what I do—I went straight to street fighting, pummeling the other student. The instructor pulled me off, and I swung at him. The Black Belt hit me, and I turned my attention to him. And, as usual, I wouldn't stop.

At first, they laughed at me—which only fueled my anger. I got in a lucky punch and wiped that grin off his face. So, he yelled at me. *Wrong move.* Shock and awe only made me angrier. *Just who did he think he was yelling at?* The next thing I knew, I was flat on my back with blood flowing from my lip. You would think that would have been enough, but when he came to help me up, I got up swinging. He hit me again and this continued until I heard him simply say, "We are going to beat this attitude out of you." For some reason, that calmed me down. This was going nowhere. I needed to learn so no one would ever beat me like this again.

We had a long discussion about lack of control and anger as signs of weakness. I didn't change overnight, and to my parent's horror, I came home a few more times in a bloody Gi—with a lip to match. But over time, I learned not only control, but to be a successful fighter, winning tournaments throughout the southeastern U.S. I would need all of this at the Academy. My first day at the Academy was a true example of the "shock and awe" approach to terrorizing an unwanted interloper.

I first saw the Academy as I crossed the Severn River bridge with my parents; I was awestruck. It was absolutely beautiful sitting back just off the river, looking like a huge castle surrounded by green playing fields. It was a combination of contemporary structures and what looked like ancient stone buildings that should be lining the streets of 18th century Rome. Atop the beige stone castle was a blue-green roof with protruding dormer windows, sloping down to encompass the top floor. Rising above all was a large dome, like the pinnacle of a typical government legislative building designed to hold the political leaders of that state or nation. This domed building was the Cathedral of the Navy, a national historic landmark, and the physical manifestation of the morality and honor expected of every midshipman. I was excited about continuing my education at this institution! Who wouldn't want to live in a castle and be educated in sleek modern structures surrounded by well-manicured playing fields?

Shock and Awe

Upon entering through Gate One, I saw Halsey Field House to the right. I separated from my family and began the process. As planned, we arrived on a rolling schedule. Outside the building were reporters and cameramen scrambling for interviews with the first class with women. Of the 1,291 plebes to arrive throughout the morning, 81 were women. *One* was a black woman. Media sought both male and female perspectives on this change to 131 years of naval tradition. I knew as the only black woman, I might draw quite a bit of undesired attention. I didn't think anything good would result from this and moved quickly and deliberately into the field house, avoiding the press.

The large, cavernous building was full of people and lights, and it seemed there was activity going on in every area of this huge athletic hall. I checked in at the table designated for last names beginning with 'M.' I was assigned my "alpha code"—a unique numeric identifier—along with my company, platoon, and room number. I was pointed to the correct assembly area and we hurriedly began our activities, which included gathering uniforms and putting on T-shirts, sneakers, name tags, and Dixie cups—our cup-shaped, blue-trimmed white hats. I met my roommates and the other plebes who were now members of my company.

Induction Day—or I-Day as it's called at the Academy—was to be a very busy day. There were haircuts, shots, and basic drill instructions. With a tightly packed afro, my hair appeared to be about 10% of its actual length, so I temporarily avoided an assault on my mane. Finally, we were taken to our summer company areas where we left our newly issued uniforms, shoes, and "gear" before reporting to another equally cavernous space. I entered King Hall, a room full of individual dining tables branching off in wings connected by a large podium in the middle. This would be the last time I was to eat in peace in this room for almost a year.

After the noon meal, the "Firsties"—or seniors, formally known as first class midshipmen—prepared us to march into Tecumseh Court—T-Court—to take the oath of office. A sea of white listened to the Superintendent welcome us and administer the oath. We were then allowed to briefly rejoin our families to say our goodbyes. I could tell my mother was concerned, and there were tears in her eyes. I kissed everyone goodbye and told them I would write and call when I could. If they had any idea of what was about to happen, they never mentioned it. I was clueless.

As plebes, we were to return to our company areas after saying goodbye to our families. We were told to "chop"—run—inside of the huge castle I saw from the bridge. It was Bancroft Hall, the gargantuan dormitory I mentioned earlier. We were to run down the center of the "passageways"—the halls—and "square" the corners, making 90 degree turns on the run as we reached silver deck plates located at each intersection. As we squared the corner, we were to yell, "Go Navy! Beat Army, Sir!" In addition to chopping through the passageways, we had to chop up the "ladders"—staircases—still squaring corners and beating Army on the way to our company areas.

Shock and Awe

With excitement and some trepidation, I finally found the appropriate wing and "deck" (floor) that held our company rooms. As I came through the swinging double doors at the top of the ladder, I was grabbed in the chest by a Firstie and shoved against the wall as he loudly proclaimed, "Black bitch, you will *never* spend the night in *my* school!" He was surrounded by a group of other white men. At first this shock and awe approach left me momentarily paralyzed. Many things ran through my mind. I could not believe in 1976, I was being physically attacked by a mob of white men because I was attending a school previously reserved only for them. I thought those days were over. Hauntingly, I remembered the lyrics from the poem, "Strange Fruit," and recalled having seen my parents driving away toward home. What it all meant to me was, I was all alone, it was too late to change my mind, and I was in big trouble.

But my final thought was, *Did he just call me a black bitch?* It was all too much to process, but those words pissed me off. That was the last thing I remember, until I came back to reality, looking down at him lying on the polished floor. The entire episode was over very quickly. I looked around at the rest of them with an undisguised fury in my voice, and asked, "Which one of you motherf*#kers wants to be next?" There was silence in the group as we stared at each other until one of them said, "Midshipman Mines, report to your room!" and pointed down the passageway. I chopped to my room.

I sensed my new roommates wondered why they were so

unlucky as to draw the "Negro card." I thought of the old Humphrey Bogart line from *Casablanca*: "Of all the gin joints in all the towns in all the world, she walks into mine." I actually felt sorry for them. There was so much to adjust to in this environment and on top of it all, they got stuck with me.

We were all moved to a different company for the academic year. I was grateful I wouldn't have to see the midshipman who attacked me—or his friends—every day anymore. It was during this June Week graduation period that something very startling occurred. When I returned to my room after their graduation, I found a vase with a single red rose and a note from him that read, "I'm sorry." I just stood there and stared at it while tears flowed down my cheeks.

Fighting men and dealing with their shock and awe approach to intimidation began as a little girl fighting older boys and later young men in my *dojo.* On I-Day, July 7, 1976, I was grateful I was not only familiar with this approach, but also capable of combating it with the tools I had developed during my youth — *No Coincidences.*

5 – *Collateral Damage*

Collateral damage is an unintended negative consequence incurred by a third party during a dispute. This can occur when others try to assist against injustice. I experienced this as a youth, and I really learned how destructive this could be as a midshipman at the Academy.

Growing up in my parents' home, there were lots of rules. At the time, they felt onerous; as I look at them now through the eyes of a parent, they made a lot of sense. (It's funny how that happens. Parents evolve from being out of touch control freaks to geniuses in the span of a nine month pregnancy. But anyway…) We had rules for what to say and what not to say; where to go and not; who to talk to and not; and when to do things and not. My parents protected us from the "boogey men" not even being publicly discussed in those days. But, in my mind, it was suffocating. From time to time, I sought ways to circumvent the rules. Much to my frustration, my parents behaved as a well-trained team, and they could anticipate my acts of rebellion before they could even be fully calculated in my mind.

Most of the time when my parents left home, my sister and I were with them or taken to stay with an older woman we called "Grandma." Both sets of our biological grandparents were deceased, and this woman served as their surrogate. As we got older, we were left with our older cousins who lived with us from time to time. The greatest opportunities for successful revolt occurred when we were left under the supervision of these cousins.

Occasionally, there were events for ministers and their wives from all the local black churches. Whenever my parents left us, they made it clear we were not to leave the house. We were not to unlock the door or set one foot outside it. If someone came to the door, we were not to answer it. And if our older cousin told us to do something, we were to obey.

The consequence for any violation of the rules was a spanking with a switch. For those unfamiliar with this weapon of mass destruction, a "switch" is a thin, wiry branch from a tree, void of leaves that may have offered padding, and knots which may have resulted in unintended harm. One could whip it with a flick of the wrist, and it would cut the air with a *swish!* The switch was the mortal enemy of all southern children. Not only were we disciplined with its stinging touch upon bare skin, but many suffered the indignity of being required to select and retrieve their own switch. I had to be pretty sure I could effectively accomplish my act of disobedience, thereby successfully avoiding this dreaded instrument of doom and gloom.

If you can imagine how frustrated I was by this "lock down" practice, it was even more aggravating for my older cousins. Not only were they aggravated by the mere fact they were required to provide babysitting duties without being paid, but this in-home imprisonment was inflicted on them as well until my parents returned.

On this particular afternoon, my parents announced they

Collateral Damage

would be back about six o'clock. They usually avoided telling us when to expect them home (for obvious reasons), but in deference to the evening plans of my older cousins, my parents shared this information so my cousins could arrange to join their friends.

Within fifteen minutes of their departure, we were outside playing in the yard with neighbor children. *What could be the harm in this?* I reasoned. I had nagged, cried, pleaded, coerced, and blackmailed our older cousins into submission. They told us we could only go out on the front porch and play alone for an hour so we had time to get back in, get cleaned up, and perform any assigned chores. The older cousins remained in the house watching television and probably napping. They didn't know we had left the porch—or that other children were in the yard.

About five o'clock we saw the big Chevy round the curb—and they saw us. The neighbor kids scrambled to get out of our yards, quickly running down the dirt path across the field separating our house from the neighborhood. We stood frozen for a moment—like deer in headlights—before we quickly ran for the door screaming our parents had returned. We didn't know what to do, but we knew we were in trouble. I contemplated just going for the switch and assuming the position, but I at least had to try to talk myself out of this situation. Not only had we been caught outside the house, but we had broken another standing rule regarding visitors when our parents were not at home.

My parents walked in the house calling our names, and we

lined up like soldiers prepared for execution. As usual, they restated the rules and the violations they witnessed. Before they sentenced us to the prescribed discipline, they allowed us to try to explain our disobedience. In my frantic attempt to avoid the dreaded switch, I not only threw my older cousins under the bus for allowing us to go out, I failed to mention their instructions for us to stay on the porch alone. In my reasoning, they were too old to get the switch, so there was no real discipline that could be inflicted on them. I could play dumb little girl who had only done what she was allowed to do.

My cousins' defense was meager, probably because they feared I would divulge the information I overheard while eavesdropping on their phone calls regarding their planned activities for the evening. (That information was *much* worse than this infraction.) I also think they felt there was not much that could be done to them. When we returned from getting our switches, I overheard a new concept called "being grounded." They were grounded for weeks, and I felt really bad about this for several reasons. I felt guilty for forcing the situation through blackmail. I felt bad the plans they made over the phone would not be executed and relationships might suffer. And finally, I knew they were going to clobber me at the first opportunity.

My cousins' freedom and relationships were collateral damage resulting from my disobedience and blackmail. I apologized, but they just stared at me like I was a mouse that had mistakenly wandered into a cathouse. I resolved to think before I opened my big mouth, to ensure others would not be hurt for situations related to my problems.

I didn't think about this resolution when I went to the Academy and informed some black upperclassmen that a white upperclassman was calling me a "nigger." I was just tired of it. As far as I was concerned, this was not just an insult to me, but to all black midshipmen. If he had only insulted my womanhood, I would not have told them. In the world I came from, if you used that term, you were subject to retaliation from *all* black people in that environment. I welcomed the opportunity to have others involved in correcting this unacceptable behavior across the Brigade. Every day, I had to chop through this midshipman's company area on a lower floor adjacent to T-Court in order to get to formation on time. He would call me "nigger," "nigger bitch," and "double insult."

I was not there when they paid the white male midshipman a visit, but I understand it got physical and the black midshipmen were punished. I felt so bad about this. They were collateral damage in my war for survival. Black male midshipmen had their own challenges, and I didn't intend to add to their problems. I wished I had never told them. Additionally, I was warned by an officer that if I told anyone what was being done to me, and they got involved, they, too, would share my eventual outcome. I was told I was on my own, and if I knew what was good for me and the black male midshipmen, I would not go running to them with my problems.

I took this warning to heart and never again told the

"brothers" about the things being done and said to me. I think most of them got the message, too, and would have been reluctant to get involved. I felt like I was at war with scores of enemy combatants—and their multitude of quiet supporters—both inside and outside of the Brigade. I had to be smart, cunning, and able to predict their attacks at all times.

I reminded myself I had powerful Invisible Friends. From this point forward, they were the go-to trinity, assisting me in defining my survival strategy and executing the plans. Some of my big brothers were supportive—or, at least, quiet. I appreciated them. There would be no more of this type of collateral damage — *No Coincidences*.

6 – *Preparation for the Future*

"You are going to college, and you are going to pay for it." My parents had made this quite clear to me for as long as I could remember. Growing up, I didn't know what I wanted to be. (In all honesty, that condition has not altered. I am still trying to figure out what I want to be when I grow up.) This level of indecision—or as I prefer to think of it, flexibility—required maximum preparation in diverse areas.

I can be very detail oriented, but I'm just as comfortable working at stratospheric levels. Micro or macro, it all depends on what level of my attention is required. I'm also very intentional about the development of both left and right brain skills and knowledge. As a child, I loved to draw, work on crafts, write poetry, perform biology and chemistry experiments with the sets my parents bought, and—much to my parents' chagrin—disassemble and reassemble electrical items.

Imagine how uncomfortable it was for someone like me to be asked questions like, "Where do you see yourself in the next five years?" or better yet, "What does success look like to you?" I have always found these questions amusing, but could never communicate my belief that anyone who thinks they have the future on "lock-down" has simply not lived long enough. Additionally, if I shared what I really thought—and why—people would think I was either nuts, some religious freak, or lacked ambition and motivation.

Please don't misunderstand. I'm not saying I don't believe

Preparation for the Future

in planning for anything. Actually, just the opposite. I believe in *prioritized* planning for *everything*! (I can see all the executive and career coaches cringing as they read this.) "It is impossible to plan for everything," one might say. This is true within the finite realm of possibilities—but I don't live in that realm. Within my realm, I want to learn as much as humanly possible. I just have to maintain the discipline to prioritize my pursuit of knowledge based upon the current responsibility.

Having said this, it is important to distinguish between "learning about" and "experiencing" as much as possible. I am definitely not interested in experiencing everything. I am very comfortable with observing others, learning as much from their mistakes and failures as I can from their successes. This allows me to cram as much information as possible into my constant state of preparation.

So how does someone who appears incapable of focusing on any one career field prepare for the future? It is based on an unquenchable pursuit of knowledge. In the third grade, I was selected for the gifted program (whatever that means). Since I had never experienced anything else, it was just normal to me. For the next nine years, there was a very prescriptive curriculum delivered by approved teachers to a very small percentage of the student body. Although this defined course load continued through high school, there were choices to be made.

Aiken High School (AHS) was a great place to go to school. It was a large 4A high school. My graduating class had over

Preparation for the Future

560 people. It was clean, safe, and orderly. Aiken County contained part of the Savannah River Site, built during the 1950s to refine nuclear materials for deployment in nuclear weapons. To meet the needs of the site, the community was inundated with advanced scientists and engineers from all over the world. The curricula in the schools were reflective of their expectations.

In the 1970s, AHS was still transitioning to full integration. Schofield High School—the black school, the "Fighting Rams"—combined with AHS with relatively little disruption. I had attended white schools since the third grade, so this process was a non-event for me. My curriculum options and the students in my classes didn't really change. (Thinking back on it, maybe they should have.)

Entering AHS through the large glass opening, to the left were neat but well-worn sofas and chairs, and to the right were administrative offices. Within this area were the guidance offices. In high school, at least once a year I met with my guidance counselor. For my first visit, my mom— the AHS head librarian—helped me prepare to discuss the classes I should be taking. Over the years, the options grew in variety and difficulty. I quickly found my "sweet spot" and my visits to the guidance counselor became very short—some were even conducted while passing in the hall! My guidance counselor knew I wanted a full schedule with academic classes every available period and comprised of the most difficult courses available. This allowed me to take college level classes in high school and prepare for

Preparation for the Future

whatever options the future held.

In addition to academic preparation to receive the required scholarships, I was encouraged to participate in any organization offering a scholarship. One of these organizations was the aforementioned Navy Junior Reserve Officer Training Corps Program. AHS had an outstanding program managed on a daily basis by a retired Marine Corps Gunnery Sergeant. He was no joke and ran a very tight ship. Upon graduation, I was the Executive Officer for the unit and was awarded an NROTC scholarship to the University of California, Berkeley. In addition to scholarship opportunities, high school NJROTC offered the unique experience of leading an organization of predominately white males in a pseudo-military environment.

Other areas of earlier preparation included my martial arts training and competitions, student body leadership positions, various academic clubs, Girl Scouts, a beauty pageant, and church organizations. Any organization or activity leading to a scholarship was on the table. As if all of this was not enough, I worked in an upscale private drug store after school and on weekends when there were not competing obligations. This was a wonderful experience that taught me how to greet and serve the public, practice business management, and foster the extreme attention to detail required for pharmacy operations. I was a very busy teenager. My efforts were rewarded as I was accepted into every Ivy League university I applied to—but I chose the Academy. I would need all of this preparation in order to be

Preparation for the Future

successful in that environment.

At the Academy, all the Do's, Don'ts, and You-Better-Not-Even-Think-About-Its were documented in a large blue binder entitled the Midshipman Held Publication (MHP). It covered everything from uniforms to the Honor Concept. All the rules, regulations, and expectations were captured here. It was the bible of the Brigade and I memorized it. It became quickly and painfully evident that the Don'ts and You-Better-Not-Even-Think-About-Its of the MHP didn't apply to behaviors targeted at running me out. I had to know when the current antagonist was in violation of the rules, so I knew how far I could go to protect myself.

The daily schedule for midshipmen is grueling, including multiple formations, inspections, memorization of rates, "chow calls," standing watches, a full academic course load (rivaling any Ivy League university), mandatory family-style meals, military training, required participation in sports, community service, and study hours. (I am exhausted just recalling this experience.) With this schedule, every moment was precious, and disruptions could quickly escalate into a domino effect of failures.

The MHP required mandatory study hours from 1930 (7:30 p.m.) to 2230 (10:30 p.m.). This time was sacrosanct and was not to be interrupted except in the case of emergency. The academic requirements dictated this time be allocated for studies only, and not to be interrupted for other activities. Studies could be conducted in the dormitory rooms, library, classrooms, or other private areas.

Preparation for the Future

Midshipmen were required to maintain a 2.0 GPA (grade point average). If the GPA was below 2.0, the midshipman could be sent to an Academic Board for review and possible dismissal.

Trying to send me to an Academic Board and "flunk" me out was part of the strategy to get rid of me. This approach should have been clean and easy. The notion that a little black girl from South Carolina had gotten in over her head and wasn't "smart" enough to graduate from the Academy would probably not even be questioned. The two-pronged approach of professor grade-lowering coupled with pressure from inside the Hall from other midshipmen should have done the trick. The study hours designated to allow time for academic preparation were the most obvious vulnerability.

"Midshipman Mines, report to my room after chow for extra military instruction." *Here we go again.* Midshipman 2/C ~~Jerk-Off~~ Doberman—a junior in my company responsible for my military "training"—was at it again. He would call me to his room and keep me there, asking questions and yelling at me while he studied—in direct violation of mandatory study hours. There were questions about newspaper articles, menus, prescribed uniforms, rank and insignia, ship types, and armament.

The most annoying questions had nothing to do with the standard rates. "Midshipman Mines, why are you here?" I always tried to avoid these conversations by sticking to the five basic responses— "Yes, sir. No, sir. Aye-aye, sir. No

Preparation for the Future

excuse, sir. I'll find out, sir."

"I'll find out, sir!"

"You don't know why you're here? I want an answer!"

I thought to myself, *You big idiot. Since you want to go there, let's go.* It was late, and he was in serious violation of study hours.

I looked directly at him. This may seem like no big deal, except plebes were to stare straight ahead, keeping their "eyes in the boat" when addressing an upperclassman, never making eye contact.

With obvious disdain in my voice, I said, "Probably for the same reason you're here, *sir*." I dragged out the word, "sir," intentionally.

He responded angrily. "I doubt that! By law, you're not allowed to do what I can do."

"*Sir*," I responded, "that was not the question. You asked why I came, not what I am allowed to do."

He was getting angrier. "So now you're a sea lawyer," he said. "You don't tell me what my question was!"

I slowly rolled my eyes back to the "boat," giving one of my five basic responses. "Aye, aye, *sir*."

Preparation for the Future

"Who do you think you're rolling your eyes at?!" he yelled, invading my personal space, which was not unusual.

I responded, "I'll find out, ~~you big stupid f*#k~~ *sir*."

Now he was two inches from my face. I glared at him and told him—without flinching—if he touched me, I would kill him. And I meant every word of it.

He knew I meant it. My reputation preceded me. *What could he do?* I thought. He was in serious violation of study hours, and I could kick his butt. The door to his room was closed—to have a junior member of the opposite sex behind closed doors was another serious violation. If he tried to give me demerits, he would *technically* have to answer for these infractions—and *technically*, his demerits would exceed mine. On the other hand, I really couldn't tell anyone. It would be a death sentence to "fry"—report a violation about—an upperclassman. *And who would I tell?* I asked myself. No one cared—or I would have collateral damages to consider. This was an uneasy stalemate, but a critical lesson for me. If upperclassmen violated regulations one on one—without witnesses—then I could fight back with no formal consequences. To say my future private interactions with Midshipman 2/C Doberman were less than mutually courteous would be an understatement.

This provocation went on for weeks, which seriously compromised my time for study and class preparation. One evening, I just stopped going to his room. He came by my room, called me to the door, and just stared. Too many witnesses. *What was he going to say?* I just smirked at him. I won this battle, but the war continued to rage. (But, that is another reflection.)

Fortunately, all of the preparation during my youth paid off. I was not overly challenged by my coursework because much of it was not new to me. Also, due to my busy schedule in high school, I made a point of learning in class and doing most of the work before I left. So, his effort to both frighten and flunk me out was not working. Although my grades didn't reflect it—due to discriminatory lowering—I was doing fine.

The moral of the story is, I chose an opportunity that didn't even exist when I was planning my scholarship options as a child. As I prepared from first through twelfth grade to "go to college and pay for it," the Academy was not on my radar screen. The law allowing the first class of women to be admitted was passed in 1975, just in time for my high school graduation. When I was approached by a local volunteer Academy "recruiter"—a Blue and Gold Officer—I asked, "The Naval *what*? What is *that*?" As you can imagine, he had an uphill battle to convince me to change my Ivy League plans for a school I had never heard of. He was successful, and I had to respect his tenacity.

Had I not prepared so broadly, I would not have been qualified for enrollment. I certainly wouldn't have been able to survive the academic landmines placed in my path. Preparation for the future entails not only pursuing known preferences, but maximizing readiness for the unknown.

Preparation for the Future

Putting all your eggs in one basket can result in a slimy mess from a single misstep. And finally, for me, I always attempt to discern God's will—and obey. That meant I had to be prepared for *any* opportunity to serve — *No Coincidences*.

7 – I Don't Care What They Think

It has always been a source of bewilderment to me why some people feel they have been granted god-like authority and powers to judge the worth of other human beings. But, I know quite a few who seem to believe this is within their purview. Since I definitely have not been endowed with these super powers, I do not judge them. I simply find them irrelevant to my self-image.

If that sounds arrogant or insensitive to the feelings of others, it's not meant to be. I listen to what others have to say regarding my behaviors or skills, thank them for their guidance and input, and adjust as I feel led. Their feedback may add to my ability to be a blessing to them, so I need to listen. Different people need different things. Being able to adjust is critical to being able to serve. Also, I care if my words or deeds cause distress for others. If this occurs, it is not my intent and I am more than willing to apologize for their distress. But, what I avoid is walking away from a discussion feeling as though I am somehow less of a person than when the conversation began.

While I choose not to assess the value of other human beings, I do understand there are some attitudes and behaviors I must either address or avoid. Again, since I'm not omniscient regarding the lives or motivations of others, I try not to judge them. Following that same logic, I refuse to allow someone else's judgment of me to impact my self-value.

I Don't Care What They Think

I learned very early in life, if you allow others to determine your self-worth, then you have abdicated to them your ability to achieve all that is within you. Many times, we assume this act to be an overt comment or gesture. Overt behaviors are easy to recognize and respond to—or not respond to, as the case may be. More challenging are the oft covert messages that bestow a value on people insidiously. This is especially impactful on children. If negative thoughts and images can be implanted in a child without detection, one is then in a much better position to predict and control the outcome of that child.

I was a little girl when I first saw this perfidious, subconscious devaluation of other human beings. My father loved to watch the evening news. My parents' bedroom was the smallest bedroom in the house, only large enough for a small bed under the double windows, a nightstand, a tall wooden floor lamp, a chest of drawers with a mirror propped on top, a small wooden chair, and a gas stove for heating. This sounds like a lot, but it was crammed into about 60 square feet with three doors taking up most of the wall space. My father would lay on this small bed as he watched the news. If I ever found him in there lying down, I would climb aboard and lay on top of him like he was a rug. So, I, too, watched the evening news.

The news was a combination of local weather, stories of interest, and any criminal activity. This evening, the pictures of two black men showed prominently on the screen. One man was arrested for shoplifting and the other for writing bad checks. Every evening, there seemed to be

I Don't Care What They Think

a parade of black men dominating the criminal news reporting. Daddy hated it when I was chatty while he attempted to watch the news, but this time I decided to ask a question that had been bothering me before I forgot. "Daddy, why do only black people do bad things?" I asked. I don't think I will ever forget his response. He lifted me and sat up so abruptly that I thought I was in trouble for talking during the news. The expression on his face looked as though someone had slapped him. He sat me in his lap as he looked down at me, and said, "Baby, black people don't commit most of the crimes. We don't even commit the worst crimes. But the news only shows the pictures of the black people. Remember when the newsman said someone robbed a bank, but you didn't see a picture? He was white."

"Yes, I remember," I said, "but because all the pictures were always of black people, I just thought they didn't have a picture of this black man."

I don't think my father realized the impact of this reporting technique until this very moment. It was typical of the double-standard he had known all his life, so much so he didn't even notice it anymore. What he had not realized was the kind of messages this one-sided reporting was transmitting to not only black children, but to all the members of the community naively taking it at—literally—face value, just as I had.

The look of determination on my father's face as he instructed me was a little frightening, but at the same time it commanded my undivided attention. My parents never talked to us about racism or ever said anything about people based on their race, so I never thought much about it. They hoped my world would be different from the one in which they grew up. This was the first of only three times in my life my father chose to make this distinction. The second was regarding the deaths of his father and oldest brother, and the last was his having to adjust to the constant flow of white boys from my NJROTC unit through his house.

"The ability to control what people believe," my father said, "will determine the future of this country, as long as people are willing to allow others to directly—or indirectly—drive their thoughts and corresponding behaviors." He shared with me how people used words, pictures, and numbers to control people's thoughts about the world around them, other people, and even themselves. He used the example of the news: based on what was shown, said, and not said, anyone might believe only black people committed crimes. Also, looking at the general crime numbers, the vast majority of crimes seemed to be committed by black people. What was not shown were pictures of white people, nor the numbers for violent and nonviolent crimes, which would have shown white people committed the vast majority of violent crimes. Additionally, the numbers failed to reflect the fact that black people were actually being charged for many nonviolent crimes, while whites received "a stern talking to" for the same offenses.

I was crushed. I didn't understand why people would do this to other people. This was horrible. *White people are bad*, I thought. My father could tell by the look on my face what I

I Don't Care What They Think

was thinking, and he further clarified his message. He told me through this negative representation, black people were being victimized and taught self-loathing, but white people were being controlled, too. In response to the now quizzical look on my face, he explained white people were being taught black people are criminals, and we should be feared. This supported the belief of black people being inferior, a ploy designed to limit interaction between the races. "They are being deprived of the opportunity to know wonderful black people," he explained, "and instead are being unnecessarily filled with fear." He cautioned I would need to be patient with white people because they, too, were being deceived.

So, a few people who control the news—and the courts—were controlling the minds of those who failed to question what they were being presented with, failing to think for themselves. "These few people," my father said, "have everyone else so focused on black, white, yellow, and red, we're too distracted to notice that they're controlling all the 'green.'"

He went on to talk about the portrayal of one of the richest and most beautiful colors in the world—black—being synonymous with evil. He explained how labeling a group of people as "black" while simultaneously showing favor to the lighter-skinned individuals within the group produced division. Defining beauty as white skin; narrow facial features; slim bodies; and bone-straight thin hair taught black people not only are we evil, but ugly, too.

I Don't Care What They Think

Holding me so I faced him, his two big hands like vice grips on each of my arms, he looked in my eyes and told me not to ever let anyone else determine my worth. "If you feel God first," he said, "and your parents are satisfied with you, don't you worry about anyone else's opinion of your worth. God's and our standards are truly very high standards to meet."

I could tell my father was facing the harsh reality that this was not the simple racism to which he had become numb, but something more deceptive and far reaching. He would do what he could. He warned people from the pulpit, reminding them as children of God they were infinitely valuable. We only played with black dolls at our house, and the picture of Jesus and the Last Supper were depicted as black. Information regarding prominent black leaders, black inventors, and all manner of black artists were readily available in my home. Most importantly, my parents spoke blessings into my life. Even in disciplining me, it would begin with the acknowledgement I was better than the infraction I committed, and they were disappointed such an excellent daughter would choose that behavior.

It was through the proactive tutelage of my parents I learned to recognize when people were trying to control my mind—and the minds of others—and that I should be equally vigilant in not permitting their success. One of my father's favorite sayings was, "It's awful hard to ride someone's back if they refuse to bend over." It was with this instruction and corroborating experiences—too numerous to detail here—I entered the Academy.

I Don't Care What They Think

The Academy is where fine, young white gentlemen are transformed into polished, expert naval officers with the honor, courage, skills to be successful in battle, and the manners and breeding to move comfortably among royalty. Young men from America's best families. This is what I was told I was destroying. The consistent message I received at the Academy was that I was only accepted because I was black and female. They presumed I was inherently flawed, and better suited to a life of servitude—not leadership.

The material in one of my STEM—science, technology, engineering, and math—classes was especially complex, but I loved it. The use of formulas and math to design solutions and drive decision-making was fascinating. The instructor in this class (I'll call him Professor Zero) seemed to be physically repulsed by me, and my presence appeared to be more change than he could absorb. He used every opportunity to belittle and humiliate me. In class, he typically ignored my raised hand, and if he *did* call upon me, he acknowledged all my answers as not only wrong, but patently stupid. When a white male classmate gave the exact same answer, the professor applauded his superior intellect and openly compared it to my stupidity. I know it was the same answer, because I read it straight from the text—and so did the other student. I would just smile when this happened because at some point, you either cry or laugh. I chose to laugh, though the instructor didn't find any humor in my response. He even walked by my desk and referred to me as a "nigger." I know the others close by had to hear it, but no one even looked up. At this point, I was

I Don't Care What They Think

numb to that word. I learned to focus on the material and ignore the environment. The material was fun.

It was a beautiful, sunny day and a crisp wind blew in off the Severn. As I walked to Professor Zero's class, I was particularly excited because we were to receive our midterm exams back. My notes had been very detailed, and I spent much of the night before the exam studying the examples and formulas. Back in those days, we performed manual calculations using slide rules and filling the pages of little blue books with complex calculations. I had no problem with the exam and anxiously awaited the results.

When I entered the classroom, there was a lot of buzz. I listened as the midshipmen discussed their predictions of the grades they were to receive. Each one was progressively more negative in their assessment of their performance. I wondered if this was a defensive mechanism so they didn't get their hopes up, or possibly some form of false modesty. Maybe it was some of both.

Professor Zero entered the room and a midshipman in the front reported the class, "All present and accounted for!" The professor immediately began commenting on his disappointment with the exam results. I thought maybe the pre-class discussions were sincere. I became concerned because I found the material so easy. Professor Zero continued to comment as he walked throughout the desks returning the exams. When he got to me, I reached for the blue book. He paused and dropped it on my desk. On the front of the book was a big, red zero. I couldn't believe it, and quickly opened the book to see what I had done incorrectly. There were no corrections in the book.

After Professor Zero finished handing out the exams, he asked if there were any questions. I raised my hand to ask why I received a zero. I was actually surprised he acknowledged me. I asked him for clarification on my grade, and he said my answers had too many decimal places. (Yes, you read correctly. My correct answers were too accurate!) I reminded him there were no instructions limiting the decimal places, and demanded to see what others had done. He told the class if anyone showed me their test, they too would receive a zero.

Imagine how demoralizing this was. I went to him after class and asked who I should go to about this. He told me I could go to hell. I figured the departments must have a leader, and I found out who this was and went to see him. He was expecting me. The conversation was very short. He told me he would raise my grade to a "B." Confused, I protested and respectfully told him I made an "A." He looked at me and said, "Professors have 10% discretion on grades based on their assessment of your officer potential." I don't know if this was true, but this injustice was the closest thing to justice I had received when seeking assistance from leadership. I just accepted it and moved on. Whether they admitted it or not, they knew—and I knew—my academic value. And more importantly, I had the knowledge. I was being provided information and skills that would prove invaluable throughout my life—they could not take this from me.

I Don't Care What They Think

Through all of this, three things were very interesting to me. First, the Academy's comfort with this type of behavior as though it were common place and institutionally acceptable. The behaviors of students and officers who found my very presence to be revolting and insulting were in stark contrast to the Academy's reputation for "fine, young white gentlemen." The language and tactics used to demonstrate their revulsion were not indicative of "fine manners and breeding" anywhere I could imagine in the civilized world. And, I was ignored or mocked by my peers and, with few exceptions, disparaged by professors and instructors. Truly exceptional behavior—*yeah, right*!

The second matter of interest to me was that people were absolutely sure I would not survive and they would likely never see me again. This belief—bolstered by the duplicity of leadership in supporting my elimination—created an environment in which no act was off limits. Midshipmen, officers, professors, and instructors said or did whatever they desired with impunity. The negative messages to me were replete with references to my inferiority and existence as a subhuman without any redeeming characteristics, whose mere presence was an insult to this fine institution.

Lastly, the most incredulous observation was they believed I would ~~give a shit~~ care what they thought! It was as though they expected some demoralized response, or for me to flee the Academy with my tail between my legs like some whipped dog. *Why would I ever seek the approval, admiration, or even basic acceptance from people who behaved in this manner?* That was the furthest thing from

I Don't Care What They Think

my mind. Their opinions of me were, again, irrelevant. I usually just looked at them, saddened by their ignorance and burdened by the uphill battle to educate them.

Although I found these behaviors curiously interesting, I did understand. My father's lessons and contextual experiences taught me this understanding. *Why would I care what they thought?* It is like accepting a hypothesis which is fundamentally flawed at its basic foundation, but to which the believers are self-righteously wed. Like trying to convince a mule with blinders on that there is beauty on every side...a mule which only acknowledges what is placed in front of him and stubbornly ignores what his other senses are telling him he may be missing. (My use of the term mule instead of jackass is both intentional and optimistic. Mules cannot reproduce with other mules and this ignorance could not perpetuate itself.) I could only pray that with time and experience, midshipmen, officers, and instructors at the Academy would reject their blinders and discontinue the destructive behaviors that reflected so poorly upon the institution which they fought so fervently to protect.

But in any event, thank God, I couldn't care less what they thought — *No Coincidences.*

8 – Angels

Have you ever experienced periods in your life when you just needed a break, longing for any small word of encouragement? Just like you, I've struggled with these feelings. The irony exists in this fact: I am absolutely horrible with receiving these gestures. Maybe I'm paranoid, seeing a pat on the back as being only one foot above a kick in the butt. Probably—and more importantly—I always felt my Invisible Friends were at the root of my successes. Accepting accolades for their accomplishments seemed disingenuous. It was equally difficult to accept blessings from angels.

Growing up in Aiken, South Carolina, everything I did worked out well. I took advantage of the outstanding education available due to the scientists and engineers residing there supporting the Savannah River Plant, the aforementioned nuclear weapons facility. I was blessed with excellent parents who taught me that manners would take me places money would not. My inquisitive nature kept me in a constant observation mode, learning as much from the bad examples as the good ones. People liked me—and I liked them—so student leadership positions came easily to me. Having said all this, I was far from perfect. I had a nasty temper. I never started an altercation, but I would absolutely decimate the opposition.

Did I mention anger was a *real* problem for me? As I shared in previous reflections, my sister and I were intermittently raised with older cousins, a boy and a girl. They were like

Angels

siblings, but because they sometimes lived with their parents in the Northeast, they were much worldlier than we were. The girl, my father's great niece, was living with him when he married my mother. My father was the youngest of his siblings and the female cousin was the grandchild of his older brother. Since my mom was thought to be infertile, she was their child. They were a happy little family unit—at least until I showed up.

Like the Academy, my cousin was not pleased with my arrival and did nothing to disguise her disappointment. I think many "only children" struggle with the birth of another child, especially if the first child was adopted into the family and the following child is biological. My cousin was five years my elder, and she wanted nothing to do with me. Except, when she felt I needed some physical harassment.

She was notorious for beating on my me when my parents weren't around. Since I was so much smaller, it was no great challenge. Having said this, she sometimes invited her friends to participate. I remember hiding in a cabinet under the kitchen sink holding all the cleaning supplies in my lap until they gave up looking for me. I didn't tell our parents because she would find a way to retaliate, even if she had to use one of her friends. Our relationship was not good, so I celebrated the day she announced she was going back north to live with her mother and siblings.

Three years later, she was back. But by then, I was older and taller than her. I was very athletic—playing football,

Angels

basketball, and softball with the neighborhood boys in our large yard. I was a strong little country girl. When she returned, I was ready to forgive and forget—but renewed harassment was not an option. I just continued with my regular routines.

On one warm, summer afternoon, I was outside playing basketball with my friends, and she asked to join us. One person on the opposing team sat out so she could play. Being the tallest, I played one-on-one defense against her, and she was unable to get off a shot. When she finally did shoot, I jumped up and batted it out of the air. Just as I was landing, I felt a slap so hard across my face my head mimicked an owl with the ability to look behind itself without turning its body. As we say in the country, *she slapped the snot out of me.*

I began to beat her unmercifully while unleashing a string of expletives that would make a Sailor blush. Blood was flowing freely, and it was as though I was recalling all the years of harassment with every strike. My older male cousin came out, yelling for me to stop, saying I was going to kill her. *Well, yeah, that was the plan.* He pulled me off of her long enough for her to stumble to the house. I managed to grab a large board—and hit *him,* so I could pursue *her.* I came inside, continuing my colorful tirade as I walked through the house yelling for her. I found her under my mother's legs as she sat on the bed. My mother sounded so pathetic that it almost amused me: "Now, Billie. Calm down, Billie." I still can't believe they didn't spank me for my language, if nothing else.

Angels

When my male cousin mentioned martial arts as a potential remedy for my undisciplined temper, my parents were happy to sign me up. I was never the instigator, but my responses to any attack were exponentially more severe than the instigating act. I could not continue to respond this way. This was a significant challenge for me until God sent an unlikely angel into my life.

My angel, my martial arts Sensei, was a middle-aged white man. I later learned he held a Ph.D. in Martial Science and was a *Judan*—a tenth degree blackbelt—the highest rank attainable in traditional martial arts. He was a World War II Army veteran with a Purple Heart, and when he spoke, people responded respectfully and immediately obeyed. He was very unassuming, a man of few words. I was the first girl to join his Aiken *dojo* and frankly, I'm not sure he knew what to do with me. He physically put an end to my temper tantrums, but more importantly, he talked to me. He was the first person to explain the vulnerabilities associated with uncontrolled anger.

My Sensei shared with me, "Anyone can lose control, but the smart person forces the other person to respond emotionally." He said if I could get them to become emotional and reactive while I remained deliberate and logical, then I owned them. He explained how losing control of my anger was not only a sign of intellectual weakness, but it made me physically vulnerable. My Sensei said that any interaction with an enemy must be calm, logical, and deliberate. I listened intently and realized these were two things I never wanted to be: weak and stupid.

Angels

I don't want to give the impression I made an immediate turn around based on his wise counsel. I was still prone to get angry: if someone hit me, I came after them with all I had. So, my Sensei used a two-prong approach. He patiently talked to me—and he thoroughly kicked my ass whenever I failed to maintain control. He also informed me this approach was not only applicable for my behavior in the *dojo*, but also applied to my behavior anywhere I found myself in life. "If I find out you're fighting," he cautioned, "the last lick will be mine." Well, I knew from experience I really needed to avoid his discipline. He taught me not to be rattled by adversaries. He said, "If you can, just walk away. You have nothing to prove." But if walking away wasn't an option, I should just turn it back on them, make them lose control and plan my response to their attack. He warned, "never engage in a fight you are unwilling to most decisively end. If you are unwilling to permanently end it, then you should walk away." His analogy was akin to not pulling out a weapon you are unwilling to use.

I am grateful to my cousin for bringing out in me a deficiency needing to be addressed. Had it not been for her mistreatment, my violent explosion, and my male cousin's repeated suggestion (as much for his sake as anyone else's)—I may have never met my angel. I was stubborn. My Sensei would have been well within his rights to toss me out of his *dojo* on the first night. But he patiently worked with me, either directly or through his other instructors, to learn control. I am eternally grateful to him.

Angels can come in so many forms. And, they usually show

up just when you need them. My plebe year at the Academy was a very lonely time. The few people I could kind of relate to were off playing their sports, or they were upperclassmen. The women were all trying to individually survive in their own ways and took little interest in me. It was like being the holiday temporary hire no one bothers to get to know very well because they believe you'll be gone soon.

I often wondered if the Academy was the right decision. At least at another school, it would not be 24 hours a day, 365 days a year of abuse. Even if the school environment was bad, at the end of the day I would have been able to leave, make friends, visit family, and have other outlets offering support. This was not an option at the Academy, so most of my free time was spent alone.

When we finally had Saturday afternoon liberty, I would usually walk out in town, alone. I always left through Gate One, the Main Gate. Outside the gate were beautiful old homes. I took a sharp left on Randall Street and headed past the old 18th and 19th century houses. I walked past the Sands House—circa 1700, believed to be the oldest house in Annapolis—on my way to the harbor. This small harbor, surrounded by plush restaurants and taverns, was an active port during the slave trade.

As I walked by the old houses, sometimes it felt as though the eyes of slave women long past just stared in awe. They had witnessed the young, white aristocratic males attending the Academy walk past their windows for over 131 years.

Angels

But, they had *never* seen anything like me before. I would imagine them running to the window and someone saying, "See! I told you so!" and another saying, "I never thought this day would come. But she's all alone, and I bet she's catching hell!" I knew they were there watching and hoping. In my imagination, I wished I could talk to them and be encouraged.

In the harbor, I thought of the slaves that disembarked and were sold through this port. All these thoughts left me with a sense of responsibility to those who endured the emotional and physical trauma of slavery. The ones who paved the way for me. The lingering spirits that chanted, *you can do it.*

I met my angel on a day like this. Just another lonely visit into downtown Annapolis spent dodging curious tourists. But the tourists were better than the locals, who made it clear they supported the men—and I did not belong. I avoided making eye contact with anyone. I didn't know what they would say or do. As I continued to walk along on Main Street, looking in windows at groups of midshipmen and tourists enjoying themselves, I noticed a little old black woman on a cane hobbling down the side street. She was trying to get my attention.

I didn't know whether to run or duck into one of the quaint shops lining the street. I was not made to feel welcome in some of those places either—I could be jumping out of the frying pan and into the fire. But these types of street interactions with the locals usually didn't go well. The side

Angels

street from which she approached angled off to the right as it slanted up the hill to State Circle. She must have seen the indecision in my body as she waved her hand for me to wait. I didn't have the heart to walk away from this wrinkled, bent black woman. It just seemed too disrespectful. She could only hurt me with words, and I was growing accustomed to that. I decided to stay there and just take whatever came.

As she approached, she looked so old, and I wondered how she could be walking these streets alone. Someone should be taking care of her. She had very dark skin with deep furrows across her face. She wore a long jacket that covered a blouse and a skirt that almost touched her ankles. What was most surprising was, she actually could not stand up straight and was not just leaning over on the cane. As she hobbled up very close to me, she turned her head to the side to look into my face. Her eyes seemed grey as though her sight was failing. I wondered how she saw me from so far away, with her bent frame and poor vision. She looked at me for a second, and then said with the wavering voice of the very old, "Baby, you know you can't quit, don't you?"

I couldn't believe what she was saying. No one had ever said that to me.

"Ma'am?"

More a statement than a question, she repeated, "Baby, you know you can't quit, don't you?"

At that moment, I felt all the slave women I passed as I walked out the gate and all the frightened slaves just landing in the harbor had found their voice through this old woman. In her bent frame, I saw the many years of struggle that had brought me to this place at this time. In her eyes, I saw the suffering of millions of people still striving to be free in a land where strange fruit hung from southern trees. It was like being shaken back to the reality that this was not about me, and how what I endured could not compare to the struggles that brought me here.

I just looked at her, and said, "Yes, ma'am."

Apparently, that answer was not decisive enough. Struggling, without a word, she continued to look up at me.

I said, definitively, "I won't quit."

Her eyes softened with a calm look resembling relief. With that, she turned to walk away. I watched her for a second—still in awe of all the feelings I had just experienced—and I pivoted to return to the Academy. I took a few steps, and then thought about her climbing that hill on her cane. I turned quickly back to see if she needed any assistance. She was gone. Maybe she had come out of one of the old buildings lining the street. It shocked me she could disappear so quickly. She was the one and only person I made that promise to. Though I never saw her again, she was a source of encouragement over the next four years. As I walked out of the gates over the years, I tried to remember to greet the spirits of the slave women watching me through

Angels

the windows of the centuries-old homes and the ones lingering in the harbor, and say, "See, I'm still here. And I hope I make you proud."

There were angels placed in my path in my youth and during my years at the Academy. Some, I never met, who worked behind the scenes to help where they could. To all my angels—seen and unseen—I am profoundly grateful
— *No Coincidences*.

9 – *Contagion*

Remember being in school when one person came in with the sniffles? If the teacher didn't intercede and send the child to the school nurse, the whole class would soon be sick. Most people are familiar with the concept of contagious diseases and how the medical community has gone to extremes to address them. Well, what about behaviors? Can they spread like a disease, indiscriminately impacting everyone they touch—even those who were not the originally intended targets?

I propose they can. If one group—or individual—is the target of a negative behavior with no corrective consequences, the perpetrator is emboldened and may inflict this detrimental behavior upon others. Most people know this intuitively. If a leader is perceived to mistreat a subordinate, the word passes quickly. If the observers share commonalities with the subordinate, they also feel vulnerable. But even those who have more in common with the leader, although less fearful, may still have a sense of discomfort. This discomfort may be attributable to the belief that the character trait allowing the leader to target certain subordinates, without remorse, has the potential to be inflicted upon anyone. In my observations, while some entities have found this type of antisocial behavior useful in ridding itself of undesirables, these behaviors tended to spread to unintended targets and later became problematic.

Every school has bullies, and mine was no exception. Quite often, they were from socioeconomically disadvantaged

Contagion

backgrounds with minimal positive parental impact. Lucy was one of these kids. She had failed to advance in her grade several times and, really, no longer belonged in elementary school. Taller and bigger than everyone else, she ruled the school through intimidation. No one was willing to report her, and the administration turned a blind-eye to her physical bullying and theft. Maybe it was overlooked because Lucy's primary targets were other poor children.

Our school was a pristine set of buildings arranged in horizontal rows, connected by covered concrete walkways and nestled in a grove of pine trees. Recess was a wonderful period of play and camaraderie on the swings, monkey bars, jungle gym, and seesaw. We all looked forward to it every day and just ignored Lucy and her latest victim.

On a sunny, beautiful day in the pines as we amused ourselves at recess, Lucy decided to expand her prey population. The latest victim would now include a new kid who came to school with beautiful jewelry, fashionable clothing, and the latest style in little-girl backpacks and lunch boxes. Her name was Tiffany. She was quiet and stood off to the side. I guess Lucy saw her as a victim too valuable to pass up. Lucy walked over to where Tiffany was standing, and pushed Tiffany against the fence, demanding her money and jewelry. We were totally shocked. Lucy had never attacked anyone outside her own demographic. Sad to say, no one really cared as long as it didn't impact them. It was well established none of Lucy's victims were willing to admit to the abuse. This tied everyone's hands in correcting the behavior. (Sound like a cop out? It was.) I and others made superficial attempts to intercede but were pushed away by the victims. Were there other courses of action available to us? Absolutely, but it wasn't our problem and we relegated our responses to commenting about what a shame it was. This all changed with Tiffany.

Tiffany was terrorized into giving up her belongings. Although she was duly threatened regarding tattling, she immediately reported it to a teacher. In her world, it was unfathomable that she should accept this kind of treatment from a Lucy. Tiffany knew she was entitled to respect. So, she reported Lucy's behavior to a teacher. This was like a bad, slow motion, suspenseful movie. We all just stood there wondering what would happen next.

We didn't have to wait long. The response was almost immediate. The teacher came to the playground and asked Lucy to come with her. Apparently, Tiffany came from a wealthy, well-respected family who was not about to let this bullying behavior continue on any level. We thought Lucy leaving the playground was the end, and we were all shocked at what happened next: interviews with the principal to discuss Lucy's behavior, not only with Tiffany, but historically. There were angry parent meetings with the school administration as to why a child as old as Lucy was still allowed to go to school with elementary-aged children. Also, why was her ongoing harassment of the children never addressed? At least, not addressed until the contagion spread to a different target—a target not acceptable to those responsible for controlling contagions.

Contagion

My parents asked, "Were you aware of the situation?"

I was ashamed to admit I was.

"Then why have you done nothing to stop what was happening?" they continued after my admission.

I gave them the weak response I had given earlier about the victims being unwilling to admit the attacks. My parents looked at me with disappointment in their eyes. I knew if my friends and I had gone to the teachers in the past, Lucy would have been corrected and Tiffany would never have been attacked.

I learned a lot from this situation. Not only are we responsible for one another, and injustice for one is injustice for all, but also unacceptable behavior spreads like a disease. Initially, Lucy's unconstrained behavior was inflicted upon the poor and disadvantaged. But this unbridled practice of cruelty grew emboldened by its conquests over the current victims, feeling no hesitation in expanding the targeted group when the motivation was sufficient. There had never been any consequences, and it was now a habit—as instinctual as breathing—because we allowed it to become an organic part of the playground experience.

This event prompted me to become a self-anointed champion of the underdog. Whenever I saw the "Lucys" at work, I would step forward to try to diffuse the situation in a way that was mutually agreeable. I learned to understand the Lucys and what motivated their behavior. I helped them whenever I could, and tried to be a bridge to mainstream them into the acceptable norms of the youth of my community. This was not always met with acceptance, but over time we learned to coexist and, in some cases, become friends. I knew we all had a responsibility to halt the contagion.

I saw and experienced bullying to an extreme that was criminal in some cases at the Academy. I was absolutely stupefied as I encountered one demeaning act or comment after another. What would motivate individuals within an organization to act out this way? I had to quickly come to terms with it, developing and executing a survival plan. What possibly could have infected some of America's best and brightest young men to behave in this manner? It didn't take long to get the answer to this question. It was a contagion.

From what I was told and witnessed, life for black men at the Academy was difficult. Many of the same accusations targeted toward women were made against them regarding their ability to lead white Sailors and Marines. Their intelligence and leadership ability were constantly under attack. Supremacist beliefs and behaviors were openly manifested by some midshipmen. I will never forget seeing people dressed as the KKK and Nazis for Halloween. All I could think was, *wow!*

I believe the women at the Academy were grateful for the support received from the black male midshipmen. We felt

Contagion

these men understood what we were going through and supported us as new members of the Brigade, struggling to find our place. Seemingly, the black male midshipmen empathized with our plight through our common shared experiences.

The Brigade of Midshipmen consisted of six battalions divided into two regiments. As mentioned previously, the black midshipmen referred to themselves as the seventh battalion—7th Batt—an organized group with officers and a treasury. I was the only female member of that battalion. On one afternoon after an always enjoyable 7th Batt meeting, I walked out with a couple of upperclassmen. I mentioned how grateful the women were for their support. One of the young men smiled so broadly, I thought his face would split and he would collapse in hysterical laughter at any moment. I stared at him trying to understand what he saw as comical in my comment. "Oh, *hell* yeah," he said, "I'm going to do *everything* I can to keep women at the Academy. You are the shit screens, the new niggers in the brigade. Life has never been so good for us."

I didn't know whether to laugh or cry. I couldn't begrudge him the look of total pleasure and relief that crossed his face. And I could sympathize. I was being called "nigger" so often, I felt they should just issue me a new name tag: Midshipman J.L. Nigger, '80. I could only imagine what it must be like for that to stop occurring, or even to significantly decrease—for whatever reason. Although many of the injustices related to being black had been heaped upon me—as well as being female—I was actually happy for him. And I knew that even though things may

Contagion

have drastically improved for the black male midshipmen, some still saw them as nothing but niggers.

So, this is where the contagion had begun. This is where the bullies—the self-appointed judges of "officer potential"—had honed their skills through harassing midshipmen they deemed to be undesirable. These undesirables were not only categorized by race, but religion could also make an individual an undeserved target. These "Lucys" had been allowed to mistreat people no one had really cared about for decades. And they continued their exploits with the first class of women, fully determined to prove women were unqualified and could not survive at the Academy.

Had these young men been required to comply with their oath of office, to obey the orders permitting minorities to attend the Academy, to understand we were all shipmates responsible for one another, to understand that through our diversity we gained a type of strength unparalleled in the world, then things would have been different for women. But the contagion that had allowed the "Lucys" to attack parts of the body of the Brigade without consequence now had a new target. Had I not personally witnessed this behavior, I would never have believed anyone would be allowed to treat beautiful, intelligent, girl-next-door, white females in such a reprehensible manner. I was dumbfounded. How far would this contagion take them? I knew if they could do reprehensible things to these white women without repercussions, my own life, here, was worth nothing. That was a terrorizing realization.

Contagion

The types of atrocities visited among some of us Academy women were criminal. *Criminal*. Some of those in leadership looked in the other direction or disciplined the woman if she protested. I felt in some ways my blackness was an advantage. I was accustomed to being called names, having opportunities taken from me, being threatened and attacked. I cannot imagine being a popular socialite, an intelligent young white woman, and then all of a sudden being treated worse than a "nigger," in some cases. These were strong, courageous young women who were victimized by a contagion that should have been destroyed at its inception.

What would America think and do if they knew what was going on behind these castle walls? Would there have been an uproar like the one that occurred when Tiffany was attacked? I wonder. These courageous women of the class of 1980 never told. What happened in Bancroft Hall stayed in Bancroft Hall. We just fought back against the contagion, developing personal antibodies that allowed us to survive.

Would this contagion follow the perpetrators to the Fleet and Corps? As the anticipated number of women increased every year, only time would tell if this unaddressed behavior would manifest itself upon the brave Sailors and Marines sworn to defend our nation.

When will we as a country realize any injury inflicted upon one part of our society will eventually spread throughout the entire body? When will we learn if the "Lucys" are not helped or addressed when they attack the less advantaged,

Contagion

they will eventually come for us all. Contagions spread —
No Coincidences.

10 – "What Did You Expect When You Came Here?"

I don't think I will ever stop initially expecting the best of people. Some might refer to that as "stuck on stupid," but I don't care. I tried to change years ago, but quickly realized my optimistic view of people is fundamental to who I am. All I can do is accept the fact that sometimes people will disappoint me, while holding steadfast to my refusal to retaliate. That would diminish me.

In all fairness, I have found people to be largely "okay." All of us exhibit behaviors from time to time that leave something to be desired. What I learned over the years is that if misbehavior is met with understanding and kindness, it has the tendency to self-correct. This has proven to be a gratifying discovery because I have had ample opportunity to experience the worst side of human behavior.

I always sought to experience the broad range of opportunities life has to offer. My criteria—if it's not immoral, illegal, or downright stupid—I was willing to give it a try. This adventurous spirit often led me to be the first woman and/or black person to engage in wide-ranging pursuits. And there is something about my perennial "stuck on stupid" spirit that always left me surprised when I was not greeted with open arms.

In my youth, I tried various activities. I mentioned my exploits as a pre-school cowboy in an earlier reflection. I

What Did You Expect When You Came Here?

also dabbled in science, mixing all sorts of incompatible ingredients, generating odors that seriously aggravated my mother. I loved the little microscopes I got in my biology sets. It was my goal to put as many things—living or dead—under the lens. That, too, did not endear me to my mom. Probably one of my most frustrating behaviors was the need to disassemble electronics and then try to remember how to reassemble them or, worse yet—improve them. I thought my mom was going to string me up when she walked into the room and saw the antenna of her new radio sitting askew. I think I still feel the sting of that ill-conceived foray into electrical engineering.

I worked in places few people like me had ever worked. I participated in activities and clubs that were traditionally male or white, but I never thought much about it. I only knew I wanted to do it. And much to my parents' credit, they never tried to discourage me by telling me all the reasons why my attempt would fail. (Although I probably could have benefitted from a "heads up" every now and then about the potential pitfalls.) I guess they didn't want to dampen my enthusiasm. It always worked out, so they just let me go for it. Sometimes, they did look at me like I was a little daft, but that didn't slow me down.

It is with this same inquisitiveness I decided to enter a pageant. Also, it offered a scholarship. I participated in almost anything that offered money for college. Based on my self-description, people may think I was not the pageant type, but I was just as "girlie" as I was a tomboy. So, when this opportunity came to my attention, I thought, *Why not?*

What Did You Expect When You Came Here?

My mother was a seamstress extraordinaire. If there was a pattern, she could make it. My sister and I had some really cute outfits, so I didn't need to worry about the clothing. I had to learn to smile until it hurt, adopting the strategic use of Vaseline on my teeth to support this effort. I practiced my walk and how to speak concisely and intelligently. My greatest hurdle was the talent competition. There were singers, twirlers, tappers, dancers, and musicians. I wasn't sure where I fit into all of this. I could sing adequately, my dance moves were only suitable for Soul Train, and earlier attempts at piano lessons had been disastrous. What I really enjoyed doing—and did well—was karate.

(Are you wondering what karate and a pageant have to do with one another? Frankly, so did I, but then—epiphany!) My style of karate consisted of two primary activities: *kumite* (sparring) and *kata* (form). *Kata* is a series of choreographed karate movements designed to display correct techniques and positions. It was like dance. And, fortuitously, there was a new song popular among my peers by Carl Douglas call "Kung Fu Fighting." (I think you can see where I am going with this. If nothing else, it would be original.)

As pageant day approached, we practiced our group activities and became accustomed to the stage and sequence of events. A few days before the pageant, we had our final rehearsal which included our "talent." I was so impressed with the other girls, and I could tell expectations were not high for my unconventional exhibition. When it was time for me to do my thing, I did as little as possible and quickly

What Did You Expect When You Came Here?

got off the stage, undoubtedly living up to expectations. I was going to need to do much better on pageant day so my entire family would not be so embarrassed they needed to leave town.

I had no delusions regarding winning. I just wanted to have fun and check this off my list. I spent the next few days thinking about my talent and how to convincingly deliver it. I didn't actually practice very much. My preparation was primarily mental. On pageant day, this paid off.

We performed our group activities and pranced across the stage, answering questions and displaying our youthful potential for all comers. The pageant was being held in a large auditorium and was very well attended. No one booed or laughed at me—a critical goal of mine—so I felt I was doing satisfactorily to this point. Most of the time we contestants were backstage getting ready for the next event, so we were not watching each other. We were in our own individual mental spaces as we listened for the applause which meant the next person was up. I waited anxiously because I knew I was next. When they sent me out to the stage in my white karate Gi, I smiled at the audience. I got on my knees and laid back flat on the floor between them with my hands in a praying position. I looked to my right to cue the music and began to rise slowly, matching the cadence of the music before I quickly transitioned to Kung Fu fighting *kata*.

I was a woman possessed. I performed every move described in the song with a flurry of kicks, chops, punches, and blocks. I didn't even know the audience was there. No one clapped or said a thing as I performed. As the song returned to its slow cadence at the end, I concluded my *kata* just as it had begun—on my knees on the floor. When the music stopped I bounced up off the floor, bowed quickly, and ran off the stage. As I was passing one of the adults that coordinated the pageant, she grabbed my arm and told me to get back on the stage. I was receiving a standing ovation! *Me?! Whoddathunk?* I ran back out, bowed again, and threw a kiss. Everyone back-stage had heard the audience's clamor, and one of the girls asked me what happened. I just shrugged my shoulders.

As the final moment approached, they gave the trophies based on personality and other areas. I won the talent award and was totally surprised and happy. But I was flabbergasted when they called me for first runner up. I know this is really the first loser, but for someone who did this on a lark, I had done pretty well. My calendar was already full and performing pageant duties would have caused it to overflow. At least, my name would be in the paper one more time. I could add these clippings to my college scholarship applications. Every little bit helped. It would have been fine, if it had ended there.

Local businesses supported the event, and it was an annual tradition for the best and brightest from the finest families in the community. As I prepared to leave, a man walked up to me, and said, "You know you won, don't you?" I didn't know what to say. He proceeded to inform me that the winner had to have a business to support her as she

What Did You Expect When You Came Here?

performed the required duties of a pageant winner. I never knew this was a requirement and no one volunteered, as I was later told could have occurred after the winner was announced. I don't know why he felt the need to tell me that I won but would not be crowned. To me, it was irrelevant and really served no purpose. Except it felt like he was saying, *Did you really expect to win?!* It felt like, *What did you expect when you came here?* In my mind I answered the unasked question—I expected the best out of everyone involved. This expectation would again be challenged at the Academy.

> *To sum it all up—as we indicated at the very beginning of this addendum—we are planning to change **very** little at the Naval Academy next year. Because, first and last, like all the rest, you will be a **midshipman**. But it'll probably take a little getting used to. For all of us. We are looking forward to it.*

This is a quote from "Women at Annapolis, Addendum to the United States Naval Academy Catalogue, 1975-76." I don't know who wrote that last line, but they obviously didn't take a poll. Or maybe it was a veiled threat, like the phone call I received to ask for my decision regarding acceptance of my appointment. I was told I would be the only black female admitted. There were supposed to be three of us, but for various reasons the other two would not be admitted. He asked with a harsh tone, "Are you still going to come?" It felt like a dare and I took it. With little hesitation, I said, "I'll be there." He paused. I think my

What Did You Expect When You Came Here?

answer surprised him. He said something equivalent to, "Fine. We'll be ready."

What had I done? Had I really just made the decision to turn down an Ivy League education—with all the benefits it entailed—to go to military school? On a dare? I thought about it and realized I probably would have made that decision even if I had known what laid ahead. I had a family tradition of service in the Army and Marine Corps. I wanted to serve my country. Additionally, this was the only true full scholarship. There would be no cost for my parents except a small fee, about $300. Everything would be provided including an outstanding education. I would even receive a paycheck. Most importantly, I would have a broader developmental experience. I would receive mental, moral, and physical education applied through strong leadership training and opportunities. I have always felt as though I was in a race with the clock to learn all I could so as to be prepared for the next challenge. The Academy served that purpose like no Ivy League school could—surrounded by the same caliber of individuals as the Ivy League—purported to be officers and gentlemen.

So, when on I-Day, I had to physically fight my way into my company area, I was shocked. I expected there would be some who would be against women at the Academy, but I never thought the sentiment would be so pervasive. It was evident in all areas of Academy life I experienced. I was not welcome and some were anything but gentlemanly in expressing their contempt for my presence.

What Did You Expect When You Came Here?

After the initial altercation on I-Day, some upperclassmen enjoyed having male plebes from other companies come to my company area for me to throw them. I would just balance them on my hip and place them on the deck as slowly as possible if they allowed me to. (Some hit the deck a little harder than others.) This was amusing to the upperclassmen, but I knew I could never fail.

It was critical I never show weakness in any area: mental, moral, or physical. At the end of the first semester, I was informed by my Company Officer that I had a 1.9 QPR—a quality point rating similar to a GPA. Since this was below the required 2.0, I could be sent to an Academic Board. I just glared at him. My actual QPR would have been higher if some grades had not been arbitrarily lowered. I gave him that, "I *wish* you would!" look. I welcomed the opportunity to have people who knew nothing about me—some of whom had never even served a hamburger—explain why they lowered my grades based on their "assessment of my officer potential." I didn't get the opportunity to say what I was feeling because he quickly clarified there would be no board. If looks could kill, he would have been a corpse.

The final straw occurred one day as I was leaving my sport alone, walking across the terrace to the dormitory wings of Bancroft Hall. A midshipman in the parking lot below yelled up at me. I didn't understand what he was saying, but I could tell by the tone it wasn't complimentary. I was also pretty sure it included my new middle name: "Nigger." I just ignored him and kept walking until I heard the sound of a rock hitting hard against the pillar right next to my

What Did You Expect When You Came Here?

head. I was ~~pissed~~ angry, and said, "~~Motherf*#ker~~ Jerk, you stay right there."

Much to my surprise, when I got to the parking lot, he was still there. He waited for me to walk in the building, down the stairs, and out the door to the parking lot. I walked up to him as he glared down at me with a "What do you think you can do about it?" expression. I had a bag full of heavy sports equipment on my shoulder, which I calmly lowered to the ground. Wrapping my hand around one end of the bag as I lowered it, I then swung it full force, knocking him to the ground. I placed my bag back on my shoulder. He still hadn't gotten back to his feet when I walked back into the Hall.

At this point, I knew something had to give. I had not made a formal complaint regarding my experiences at the Academy. I understood the concept of the chain of command. I knew the midshipman chain was unresponsive, but I was sure the officers—older, wiser, and resplendent in uniforms bedazzled in gold—would be shocked and take action. Naivety strikes again…

When I mentioned my concerns, I was again surprised by how quickly I was moved up the chain until I stood before a senior leader. It was as though the lower officers were instructed to just pass me along without comment. Maybe they thought they finally had me on the ropes, and I was ready to throw in the towel. If not, this meeting was sure to push me over the edge. As I walked into the beautiful office, I was asked why I was there. I had practiced my speech so

What Did You Expect When You Came Here?

as to be as respectful and concise as possible in expressing my concerns regarding physical attacks, grade lowering, and racial slurs. The senior officer just stared at me as I delivered my rehearsed monologue.

I was still standing in front of his desk when I finished, having never been offered a seat. He looked at me and said, "What did you expect when you came here?"

I don't remember much of the details after that comment, except he made it quite clear these issues were *my* problems, and if I couldn't deal with them, I should leave. Finally, I smirked at him as I firmly communicated that I would deal with it, but I had just felt responsible to provide the Academy the opportunity to live up to its reputation. He didn't like that response and told me to get out of his office. There would be no further guilt when I did whatever it took to survive. I realized those in the Brigade who felt personal responsibility to get rid of me could act without consequence. Sometimes you just have to meet people where they are.

The senior leader's response forced me to employ all the lessons of my youth in order to survive. My Invisible Friends, independent spirit, intense preparation, and the wisdom of the angels would all be leveraged to mount a counter-attack while at the same time minimizing collateral damage. As he said, "This is your problem." No one else should have to suffer on my account. At least those who didn't deserve to suffer.

What Did You Expect When You Came Here?

That question, "What did you expect when you came here?" significantly impacted the person I became. I thank that senior leader for failing to live up to my expectations. He taught me some important life lessons. As far as I was concerned, it was a no-holds-barred fight to the death with all comers. In a future that crossed 14 industries and many organizations, I never faced anything I was unprepared to deal with. I had multiple options available to address any issue. Thank you, Sir — *No Coincidences*.

11 – Use What You Have

Life gives different gifts and circumstances to us all. Some have significant material assets, or a superior mind, or wonderful parents, and so on. Some of my friends growing up were quite wealthy—lots of money and travel. It's tempting to focus so much on what others have, that we fail to fully appreciate and use what we have.

Let me share a little about my home town. The municipality of Aiken was incorporated on December 19, 1835, forming around the terminus of the South Carolina Canal and Railroad Company—a rail line from Charleston to the Savannah River—and named for William Aiken, the railroad's first president. Among its founding commissioners, during the short-lived Reconstruction Era, were three African-American legislators: Prince Rivers, an escaped slave, Union soldier, mayor, and one of the first black judges in the state of South Carolina; Samuel J. Lee, State Speaker of the House and the first black man admitted to the South Carolina Bar; and Senator Charles D. Hayne, a member of Charleston's elite families, who served in the Confederate Army and as postmaster. Aiken was a planned town, with many of the streets in the historic district named for other cities and counties in South Carolina. In the late 19th century, Aiken earned distinction as a wintering spot for wealthy Northeasterners, leading to the Aiken Winter Colony being established by Thomas Hitchcock, Sr. and William C. Whitney. Over the years, many famous and notable people 'wintered' in Aiken, including Louisiana Senator James B. Eustis, socialite Madeleine Astor, philanthropist William Kissam Vanderbilt, president of Bethlehem Steel Eugene Grace, Secretary of Commerce W. Averell Harriman, and many others.

In 1950, the federal government asked DuPont, one of the largest and most prominent chemical production companies in the country, to build and operate a nuclear facility near the Savannah River in South Carolina. DuPont had expertise in nuclear operations, having designed and built the plutonium production complex for the Manhattan Project during World War II. On November 30, 1950 the U.S. Atomic Energy Commission announced the selection of a site near Aiken to build a thermonuclear weapons fuel production plant.

In the early 1950s, working in the Savannah River Site, Frederick Reines and Clyde Cowan developed the equipment and procedures necessary to detect the once undetectable neutrinos, as confirmed in the July 20, 1956 issue of the publication, *Science*. Forty years later, Reines was awarded the 1995 Physics Nobel Prize. Cowan had already died.

Born in Newberry, South Carolina—that's where Grandma lived—I soon went home to Aiken in 1958. During my youth, Aiken was at the peak of its nuclear science and technology growth. Imagine the people that flowed through this small town and what they demanded of the school system. As mentioned earlier, I benefitted greatly from their influence attending advanced classes alongside their children.

Use What You Have

Although their world was different from mine, I shared a thirst for knowledge with my classmates. I was acquainted with almost everyone, but I let very few people into my life. In a town like Aiken, there were several groups; the "haves," the "have nots," and the "haven't gotta clues." I was in the latter group. Even though I was surrounded by wealth, for some reason I never focused on the comparison.

I was the one who always went up to the new kid or the misfit and got to know them. These wealthy, nerdy children usually fell into this group. My best friends growing up were people I met this way. I think I preferred them because they usually shared the same behavioral limits my parents imposed on me. (If there were certain things I couldn't do, why would I surround myself with people who do those things? That would be a recipe for disaster.)

Kathy was one of those people. She lived on a huge estate in town. I went to visit her, and she didn't just have her own room, but a suite of rooms—all to herself. Her rooms were clean and orderly but felt cold to me. It felt more like a hotel than a home. Her parents traveled a lot, so she had a nanny. She was so nice. Kathy was small and thin and possessed a wonderful personality she hid from others. Even though I was surrounded by all this wealth, I said, "This is nice. Wanna go to my house?" She enthusiastically agreed. We got permission from the nanny and called my mother to pick me up. Although my mother must have wondered why my visit was so short, she said nothing except that she was on her way. I could tell she was surprised when Kathy jumped in the car, too. I forgot to mention that part. Mom confirmed parental permission and we were off to my house.

To put it mildly, I didn't live on an estate. As mentioned, I lived in a white cinder block house in the city—but back down a dirt road—on the prettiest two acres of land you ever wanted to see. There were beautiful flowering plants, fruit trees and vines, a large vegetable garden, and land cleared for play. The house had two porches, and inside there were three bedrooms, a living room, dining room, den, and large kitchen. On the other side of the garage, my father connected a small house which he moved onto the land—a 70's version of a man cave. The furnishings were modest and clean, and the kitchen was very basic with handmade cabinets and mix-matched appliances, but it was full of the most tempting aromas, and lots of love.

The main part of my house was about the same size as Kathy's personal quarters. I never thought about being envious of what Kathy had. My experiences with my well-to-do peers taught me there were a lot of lonely children behind those manicured lawns. Mothers who drank to compensate for feelings of inadequacy, fathers who never came home, or parents who traveled and spent very little time with their children. Or worst yet, parents who were there—but not there. Kathy spent a lot of time at my house while we were growing up, but we eventually grew apart as the temptations of unsupervised wealth drew her into a world I was unwilling to enter.

What I had were parents for whom their children were the center of their lives. They were never discouraging and

Use What You Have

always made us feel as though we could accomplish anything. What resources they had were allocated to their children. They never traveled without us, exposing us to as much useful information and experiences as they could. They were intimately involved in every aspect of our lives. Privacy was an unheard-of concept. "If you have nothing to hide, then there is no need for privacy," they said. All they required was excellent behavior and great grades. We had everything we needed and most of what we wanted. If I had focused on Kathy's advantages, I could have missed the value of what I was provided, and followed her into a life of drugs.

It can be so easy to be distracted by the perceived advantages of others. We fall into negativity and doom ourselves to failure— or at best, mediocrity—based on our own attitudes. We are often so concerned with the connections, resources, looks, birthright, etc. of others, we are unable to focus on using what we have. I leveraged all my "haves" to obtain every academic opportunity I pursued, including my appointment to the U.S. Naval Academy. I would need to continue this approach to maintain my focus there.

Have things ever been so difficult that you would have been happy just to get a bone? It wouldn't even have to have a lot of meat—just happy to gnaw on the gristle and suck out the marrow. I definitely felt that way at the Academy, especially during the first two years. If I could have just gotten a break—any break—it would have elicited from me such gratitude, the giver would have said, "Really?

All that for a bone?" What I *couldn't* do was focus on what I *didn't* have, and especially not compare that to others.

The Academy, like many other established academic institutions, made every reasonable attempt to support "legacies"—a direct relative of a graduate. This was not merely a show of favoritism, but it was taking advantage of families that were proven commodities in terms of national and military service. The Academy is a difficult place for most midshipmen, so a person whose family can prepare and support them through the journey tends to be successful. Given this initial advantage of active family support, the probability of success was significantly enhanced based on the level of success of previous family graduates. Simply put, if daddy was an Admiral, member of Congress, magnate of industry, and/or filthy rich making significant contributions, the "legacy" midshipman would have to hang the Superintendent upside down from the flagpole—in his skivvies, with a tutu on his head, in a raging snow storm—in order to fail. I wonder if his grades would have been lowered based on officer potential?

Another special status category was the recruited, high-performing athlete. I don't begrudge these individuals their perks because the grueling Academy schedule is not at all conducive to successful NCAA championship performance. The training schedule and competitive events—on top of carrying 18 to 24 credit hours of primarily science, technology, engineering, and math—in addition to all the military training requirements would be overwhelming. In order to accommodate the athletic rigors,

Use What You Have

these midshipmen sat at separate tables where they could eat in peace, were permitted to register for classes earlier than the rest of the Brigade to avoid the more difficult instructors, were allowed exemption from military training (or at least a streamlined version), among other coveted benefits. In return, they generated huge amounts of funding to support the Academy mission and were outstanding recruiting emissaries.

And then there were those who had so much money they raised retail therapy to an art form. They had beautiful clothing, jewelry, shoes, electronics—everything a midshipman could have but only the best. Their cars were a testimony to their resources as well as their extensive travel itineraries during all leave periods. Also, their parents' contributions gave them a level of access few other midshipmen even knew existed.

I had none of these advantages, but what I had was obviously more than adequate. And just like with Kathy, I was not envious of other midshipmen. My experiences in Aiken taught me all that glitters is not gold, and it is a worthless pursuit to focus on the perceived advantages of others. I had great intellect, strong values, outstanding parents, a never-give-up perspective, and most importantly Invisible Friends. I used all of this to my advantage.

I had no interest—or time—to look back and focus on how I was treated a minute ago, and even less interest in the benefits someone else was receiving. My concern was the challenge to be faced in the next minute regarding the threat

Use What You Have

around the next corner. The ability to "keep it moving" and avoid distractions were also valuable traits I possessed.

During my youth, I learned success was not based on what I had or didn't have. It was based on what I did with it. In an environment where so much was denied, I learned not to focus on the denial, but instead to maximize my benefits, striving to be the best I could possibly be in every aspect of my life—including being a blessing to others — *No Coincidences*.

12 – Silent Majority

The phrase "the silent majority" was in use for much of the 19th century to refer to the dead. The number of currently living people is actually less than the number who have died throughout human history. In 2011, there were approximately 14 dead people for every living person, so the dead were the majority in that sense. Today, it refers to living people who behave as though they are dead when they witness injustice but fail to act. Albert Einstein said, "The world will not be destroyed by those who do evil, but by those who watch them without doing anything."

I grew up on westerns. Anyone familiar with the genre knows they are morality plays responsible for teaching an entire generation of Americans right from wrong. The characters reinforced the teachings of my parents and were always there to help their fellow man: The Cartwrights on the Ponderosa; the Barkleys in the Big Valley; The Virginian on the Shiloh Ranch in Medicine Bow, Wyoming; Slim Sherman and Jess Harper from outside Laramie, Wyoming; John and Victoria Cannon of the High Chaparral Ranch in the Arizona Territory; the Ingalls family in the Little House on the Prairie; and of course, John Wayne—"The Duke"—*wherever* he was.

My father always preached, "The crowd will lead you straight to hell." He preached Matthew 7:13, "Enter through the narrow gate. For wide is the gate and broad is the way that leads to destruction, and many enter through it." He really drilled this point home, and my western heroes

Silent Majority

demonstrated the ability to enter through the narrow gate and save the day—all in less than 60 minutes. I learned if you ever find yourself on a crowded road, in harmony with all the other travelers, check your map—you are probably off course.

I was a young child as I watched the civil rights protests on the television with my father. Due to the unique nature of my community—a geographically diverse and highly intellectual population—many of the issues being protested were not overtly obvious in my world. But my father preached about the importance of the movement and participated in voter registration drives. He and other ministers, spoke out against civil rights violations when they occurred, usually quickly resolving the issue.

On television, I watched people beaten with batons; innocents attacked with high pressure hoses; and dogs rip into the flesh of men, women, and children. All these atrocities were being perpetrated by a relatively small group of men. The attackers were usually policemen or white supremacist groups. It was often difficult to distinguish between the two based on behavior. History repeated itself as most people stayed in their homes feigning ignorance, demonstrating quiet support, overcome by fear of personal consequences, or showing complete apathy—the silent majority.

Civil rights conditions did not improve until more members of that silent majority joined in the protest. They were those people who couldn't just sit in front of their television screens and watch their fellow man being victimized for demanding the basic liberties others took for granted. They found their voice and made a difference. Some of them paid with their lives. My father always pointed these courageous people out to me, and I am eternally grateful to them. They were the people I wanted to emulate. However, the silent majority encompassed the vast majority of the midshipmen at the Academy.

My strategy was one of invisibility and unpredictability. If I was not required to be in a specific place at a specific time, I hid. You cannot harass what you cannot find. The harassers were actually small in number and most of them were careful not to have an audience. Whether the harasser was alone or in a crowd, avoidance was my tactic. Confrontation wasn't worth it. I just hid.

Hiding was not always an option. There were certain places we had to go and usually between certain hours. I got smart and learned to vary my route if possible, but the destination was the same. For example, the only phones available to plebes were located in a room with a bank of phones. Usually during mealtime or between scheduled activities were the best times to use the phones. This was an opportunity to talk to people outside of the Academy who loved me, a time to share some of the challenges of the day. Somehow, the vocal few always knew when I was coming. I guess it was pretty predictable. The plebe schedule was tightly orchestrated. By the time I finished reciting my rates, there was no time left to call home. I don't think they were supposed to do that; others passed by and either

Silent Majority

laughed or said nothing. I stopped calling home. I also stopped writing. The mail chutes were right in the middle of the company area—I would be like a deer in an open field in broad daylight during hunting season if I tried to mail a letter. These were lonely times. There was a price to be paid for hiding.

Unfortunately, there was nowhere to hide in transit to classes. Outdoors, plebes had to walk on the straight walkways. This meant right down the middle of the campus. Upperclass midshipmen could use the curved walkways bordering and intersecting the main walkway—Stribling Walk. I tried to make these transitions as quickly as possible because several times I was narrowly missed by rocks. They were usually thrown pretty low and designed more to harass than injure. It always hurt my feelings more than my body. Whenever I looked in the direction of the rock's origin, there was usually a group of people just standing, looking back at me. Only one threw the rock, but the others gave their tacit approval through their silence.

Although I couldn't always hide, I did have several effective hiding places. Most frequently, I was either in the catacombs or the Jewish Chapel. The catacombs were kind of creepy, and there were mice in those spaces, so my favorite hiding spot was the Jewish Chapel. That's right—chapel. I know Jews do not have chapels—they have synagogues. But at the Academy, there was a chapel. The Jewish Chapel was a medium-sized storage room located on the First Regimental side above the Rotunda. Very few people knew it was there. The room was labeled "Supplies."

Silent Majority

It was a carpeted room with a few rows of chairs. In the front was a podium and table. The far wall was made from a beautiful, dark wood, maybe mahogany. Inlaid in the wood was a large star of David engraved in gold. The lights were usually low, but bright enough to study. Most of the time no one was there, but sometimes there would be a few Jewish midshipmen in the room. If there appeared to be any religious service in progress, I would leave. I really wanted to stay and learn, but I didn't want to intrude. When there were no services, I would quietly sit in the back and—although they ignored me—I never felt frightened or unwelcome. I was grateful they shared the space—and their silent acceptance. Sometimes, silence is golden, but not when it enables injustice.

I have received many apologies since graduation. I was often clueless regarding the offense that occurred. It was many years later when I realized the apologies were for what they had *not* done. They apologized for being a part of the silent majority. I fully accepted the apologies. The kind of strength required to stand against the raging tide of disapproval of women midshipmen would have been uncommon. This individual would have opened themselves up to receive the same treatment as the women—like the collateral damage.

It would not be truthful to say no male midshipman ever spoke up. Occasionally, someone would say, "That's enough," ending the current inappropriate act. But it was like the parent who constantly tells the toddler to stop. There is usually a brief acknowledgement, but the toddler soon returns to the misbehavior because it knows there is

Silent Majority

no real consequence. And fundamentally, the toddler doesn't understand *why* he should stop. Although the brief respite was appreciated, it only gave me the *opportunity* to hide. It didn't end the *need* to hide. But at least the midshipmen was not silent.

Only once do I remember hearing about a midshipman with a position of authority stating the mistreatment of women was unacceptable and was to end immediately. He explained the female midshipmen were here for the same reason as the males. It was not our fault the law had not caught up with us yet, but when it did we would have women ready in the pipeline. He said the girls were to be treated no differently than the guys—and if anyone had a problem with that, they would answer to him. I am sure he was not the only one. At least I hope he was not. But he did become like a mythical urban legend. Decades passed before I found out who he was, and I had the opportunity to say thank you for not being part of the silent majority — *No Coincidences*.

13 – "What Is Your Objective?"

Being a parent is a difficult endeavor. I know that now. My parents were fully consumed with developing and protecting their children. We needed look nowhere else but to God for support of any kind. They made sure we saw them as the source of all our needs, both emotional and physical. They never turned over our education on any topic to anyone else. This included academic, moral, and physical. They were involved in it all and monitored us closely. One of these mundane—although very important—tasks was driving.

In South Carolina in the 1970s, a driver's permit could be obtained at age fifteen and a driver's license at sixteen. I drove the car around the yard for weeks before my father mustered up the courage to take me out on the road. I drove with the same passion I lived. Remember that whole anger management issue? It followed me behind the wheel. Not to the extent I would use the car as a weapon, but I would throw a major hissy fit behind the wheel if I felt disrespected. Occasionally, my middle finger was used for more than scratching my nose. Thanks to my father's patience and prayers, I earned my driver's license. My parents rewarded this effort with a brand new Pinto station wagon. There was now a new driver on the road with more than her share of attitude.

What really enraged me, and what I think was at the root of my issue, was when another driver looked in my face and then decided to just cut me off, pass me and throw on the brakes, or do other stupid things like that. Again, I never started anything. I was the friendliest, most giving, caring person you could ever meet. I would wonder if people looked at me and saw this side and decided to take advantage. As a fierce champion for the underdog, I found bullies reprehensible. When they chose me as a target—mistaking kindness for weakness—I made them pay. It took major restraint to curtail this behind the wheel.

After a particularly difficult day at high school and after-school club activities, I was in no mood for bullies or bigots. A dysfunctional teacher had made class particularly difficult this day. (It's interesting how easily a teacher can manipulate children's minds, both positively and negatively. We can carry perceived limitations against or in favor of particular subjects based on our experiences with a teacher.) I was in a very bad mood and had reached my limit of passive-aggressive behavior for one day. I completed all my school assignments and needed to get to my job by 5:00 p.m.

The intersection of Laurens Street and Hampton Avenue could be particularly treacherous. In a small town, ten lanes came together at a red light with an oblong, zig zag intersection. Traveling in the north-south directions, the intersection was long and the expected path for turning vehicles was to pass and turn behind each other. Due to the length and irregular shape of the intersection, to cross in front of one another could easily lead to an accident.

On this particular evening, I was on a mission. I had about five minutes left before I was to be behind the cash register at work. Have you ever looked across an intersection, or in

What Is Your Objective?

the window of the car next to you, saw someone looking at you and could tell it was a challenge? That is how this woman looked at me and I was not having it!

My route was straight ahead, and she wanted to turn left in front of me. I had the right of way, so if I hit her it would be her fault. She would have to be stupid. *Whatever,* I thought, *it would be on her.* I waited for the light to change with my foot hovering over the gas pedal, determined to go straight forward at full speed. I was in the right, and I was not going to be disrespected. Not again. Not today. After what felt like an eternity, the light finally turned green. I slammed on the gas as did the small, green sedan across the interstate. *This idiot was still going for it!* My front end was barreling down on the rear passenger door as I slammed on brakes. A small head peeped up so only half the face was visible. My car came to a screeching halt as the green car flew by. She risked her child's life in order to win some insane challenge.

And I was just as crazy as she was. Yes, right was on my side, but I could have been *dead right.* Worse yet, I could have killed a child all because I lost sight of my objective. I just needed to be at work in the next few minutes. I let the injustices of the day—and one more stupid challenge—pull me off course with what could have been disastrous results. It's easy to get caught up in the current challenge of the day, losing sight of the longer-term objective. At the Academy, I had to swallow my pride many times when I felt injustice and maintain focus on my objective. As we said, "Cooperate and graduate."

What Is Your Objective?

Physical conditioning was a large part of midshipman training. We did sit-ups, pushups, pull-ups (or hangs), and timed runs. Halsey Field House was where we gathered for testing. On this particular day, we were dropped off at the field house for our physical fitness tests and told to report back to our company areas after completion. The first class midshipmen responsible for monitoring the tests were spread out at different stations to observe each individual event. We counted and reported the results for each other as we completed each event.

Previously, I had done pull-ups, but women now had the option of doing the flexed arm hang from a bar, keeping our chin above the bar for a prescribed period of time. I preferred the flexed arm hang to pull-ups, as it came quite easy to me. I always tried to max out the pushups and usually came pretty close. But sit-ups were the bane of my existence. The exercises I did in martial arts were very different from what the Academy required for testing. Although I had rock hard abdominal muscles formed by allowing almost 200-pound men to walk on them, sit-ups were difficult and painful. During this fitness test, I started out quickly with one sit-up repetition after another, my fingers laced tightly behind my head. As the time limit approached, I strained to complete a few more sit-ups and my fingers began to loosen. As I jerked forward one final time, my hands slipped from behind my head as my fingers came unlaced, and my head snapped back against the hard floor. I heard a loud pop and pain seared through my neck. I yelled out and actually saw lights before my eyes as I rolled over into a fetal position. I couldn't move. My neck hurt so bad it could no longer support my head without excruciating pain. I scooted over against the wall, waiting for my classmates to finish the run.

After all the tests were finished, the plebes fell into formation by squad and a Firstie from our company came to escort them back. My squad leader was not with them. The Firsties who were in charge of the testing told them to go ahead and leave, and I would follow shortly. I was still crouched against the wall in pain. After all the other midshipmen left, the two remaining Firsties focused their attention on me. They yelled at me to get up and run around the track. I tried to explain how my neck hurt, but they just continued to yell.

I used the wall to prop myself up as I slid my body up it, balancing my head by placing my thumbs under my chin and placing my hands on both sides of the back lower-half of my head. I could barely walk, and these guys were yelling at me to run—or get out of *their* school. The requirement was to run one mile, four laps around the indoor track. I staggered to the track and tried to run. Each step felt like I was being stabbed at the base of my skull. I couldn't see straight and staggered from one side of the track to the other as I tried to make it around. After one lap, I knew I was about to pass out, but I was terrified of what would happen to me if I did. I was all alone in the field house with these guys who didn't want me in *their* school.

I stumbled back to the wall close to the end of the bleachers. I slid down the wall as they continued to stand over me,

What Is Your Objective?

yelling at me. I tried to drag myself under the bleachers. There was so much anger in their voices. I couldn't fight back. I was terrified. Then I heard the most wonderful sound in the world. My squad leader had come back looking for me. He must have suspected something because his breathing indicated he had obviously been running to get to the field house. He walked in angrily, yelling at them, "What the f*#k are you doing? Get away from her!" They started to reply, but they could tell he was in no mood for conversation, and the situation could quickly become physical if they didn't back off.

He asked me if I was okay, and I explained—between gasping in pain—I had hurt my neck doing sit-ups. As he reached for me under the bleachers, he asked if I could walk. It was so hard to focus on his words. I just wanted to lay still and not be in pain. I wanted to go to sleep. He was much taller than me, but he put his arm around my waist and told me to lean on him. I took a couple of steps, and I don't remember anything until I woke up in sick bay.

Bancroft Hall had its own medical clinic to deal with the day-to-day injuries and illnesses of the Brigade. If the condition was serious, there was also a full in-patient hospital fully equipped for surgery called Hospital Point. I don't think I was taken to Hospital Point. I just remember being helped back to my room with a huge neck contraption attached to my shoulders, supporting my head and not allowing my neck to turn. I was assigned bed rest and wore the brace for about two weeks before transitioning to a soft brace that allowed me to turn my neck. It took months to

What Is Your Objective?

fully heal. Almost none of this was documented in my medical record.

My squad leader came by my room to check on me. I was feeling better and thanked him for coming for me. I could tell he was bothered by the entire situation. I asked him if they could do that to me. I was angry and wanted to make them pay. He said I could put them on report, but I should think about what that really meant. At the Academy, plebes didn't put Firsties on report. A charge like this could result in their dismissal—if anyone cared—but it couldn't be swept under the rug. I told him I could go to the media. He looked at me for a while—saying nothing—and finally said, "You can do that. But, what's your objective?" Still in pain and not quite understanding his point, I asked what he meant. He said, "Do you want to get revenge and punish them, or is your objective to graduate?"

That may have sounded like a cold statement, but it was the truth. If I had caused them to be expelled and sent to the Fleet as enlisted men, not only would most of the men in the Brigade have made it their personal mission to run me out, but all women would suffer. He didn't have to say all this. I knew it without him even saying it. Seeking revenge was a lose-lose situation. I had to leave their consequences to my Invisible Friends, focus on getting better so I could protect myself, and graduate.

I learned to beware of distractions. Once I was sure of my objective, I couldn't allow myself to be sidetracked by the words, actions, and behaviors of others. I couldn't lose sight

What Is Your Objective?

of the objective while trying to address every perceived injustice. You will never hit the target if you can't focus on the bullseye.

At the Academy, my goal was graduation. If I could open some minds along the way, that would be great. But nothing would open more minds than my graduation. I would not be distracted from my objective — *No Coincidences*.

14 – Hold Your Tongue

Okay, I admit it. I struggled to keep my mouth shut. The scripture my parents had me recite at every Sunday morning meal was, Exodus 20:12. "Honor thy father and thy mother that thy days may be long upon the land that the Lord thy God giveth thee." Yes, *every* Sunday, for over a decade! That same scripture, over and over again. I guess this happened because I was a little slow in getting the point. *Or, maybe I just couldn't help it? Naw, that wasn't it.* The problem was I had no patience for conversations I considered useless.

Growing up, if someone said something to me I considered unintelligent or illogical, I basically replied with a curt response, communicating my conclusion and moving on. In hindsight, it came off as condescending and dismissive. That was not my intent. Often, if I thought a comment was absurd, I responded with the obvious solution or counterpoint, and thought nothing else about it. I was not trying to be a smart-ass. And I didn't start these conversations. Adults seemed compelled to walk up to me and say dumb things. *Why?* I don't know. And again, it was not my intent to be disrespectful. Half of the time, I was speaking more to myself than to them. When they looked at me aghast, I usually said, "Oops, did I say that out loud?"

Unfortunately, my auto-piloted tongue resulted in people thinking I thought they were stupid. This wasn't true. I spent no time judging them. I was just responding to the singular comment. What probably exacerbated the situation was that what I was saying was so fundamentally true. If they thought before speaking, they probably wouldn't have made the comment. I behaved like this as a very young child. (Yes, this issue started early.) My dad said I was an old soul. I don't think so, I just listened—even when they thought I wasn't listening—and repeated back to adults what I had heard them say. Usually, situation appropriate. I had no reason to believe what I was saying was impudent. Especially because, not being very talkative, I didn't voluntarily interject my thoughts. I was simply responding to comments.

I guess it's even more frustrating when small children use your own words to correct you. My poor mom, she got more than her fair share of this from me. She was a very emotional person who unfortunately gave birth to R2-D2, the Star Wars robot. I was a small, logical creature. The fact I bonded well with men and learned a lot of their less sensitive communication styles didn't make it any better. Due to family medical issues, I missed the opportunity to bond with my mother, so she tended to take my comments personally. (You are probably thinking, *Well, yeah, you said it to her personally, so why wouldn't she take it that way?* Touché. Point taken. But I didn't mean it that way.) Since disrespect wasn't my intent, I just assumed people knew that. The tactlessness of youth. But my mom just seemed to always ask for it.

Like most parents, mine would occasionally argue. Mom was the one who tended to escalate the disagreement, probably because she felt she wasn't being heard. My parents always said grown-ups should not have adult conversations around children. My mom would speak so loudly, I couldn't help but hear the disagreement. Most of the time, I thought it was over silly stuff. In any event, I was not having it. So, what was my response? I would scream, "Stop! I don't need to hear this!" And they would either stop or go someplace else and speak more quietly. They had their issues, and I had no patience for being involved in them, directly or indirectly. The last time my mother involved me in her relationship with dad, she never repeated that mistake, due to one of my more pointed responses.

My parents had separate bedrooms. Sometimes they slept together and sometimes apart. My mother's room was actually relatively large, and the entire family spent a lot of time in there. The room was probably about two hundred square feet with hardwood floors and a large double window that framed a backyard containing fruit trees and grape vines. The furnishings included a full-sized bed and a twin bed, a dresser with mirror, and a large chifforobe—a combination wardrobe and chest of drawers. The room was heated with a small gas heater. We often all lounged in this room, talking and watching television.

On one of the days my mother was even more frustrated with my father than usual, she expressed her concerns to the children. My sister and two cousins were sitting on the full-sized bed near my mother, and the group was commiserating with her regarding all her perceived injustices. The discussion even progressed to discussing separation. They all quickly exclaimed that if my parents

Hold Your Tongue

separated, they would live with mom. My dad was in the den watching television. I could see him through the open door, and I knew he could hear this. But he behaved as though nothing was going on.

He actually had done something for which her anger was justified but, in my opinion, not enough to leave. (I know you want to know what he did, but that's "Nunna ya bizness." You know too much already *(smile)*. Okay, back to this reflection…)

I sat alone on the twin bed ignoring them all. I was—and continue to be—a drama-free zone. If someone wanted to have an emotionally volatile argument with me, they would quickly realize it was a one-way communication. Just as I would confront my parents about having arguments in front of me, I also wouldn't participate in these emotional exchanges. Logical discussion with no drama was what I preferred. The discussion across the room seemed useless to me. I didn't yet understand the process of venting. In fact, it took another sixteen years for me to comprehend the difference between talking for release and talking for solution. In any event, I wasn't going anywhere, and neither were my parents. There would be no separation.

As I sat there watching television, I noticed the room had suddenly become quiet. I looked across the room and noticed everyone was looking at me.

"Well?" my mother said.

Hold Your Tongue

"Yes, ma'am?" I answered. "Well, what?"

"I know you heard us talking," she said. "You haven't said anything. What do you think?"

I looked at her and said, "You decided to marry him without asking children. I don't think children should be asked about what you want to do now. You need to be talking to my daddy."

If looks could kill, I would have expired that day. I think she even threw a shoe at me—I ducked and left the room. The others came out soon afterwards, and I never heard anything about it again.

I was not being purposely disrespectful. I was repeating what my parents taught me. I was just a blunt child. As I was preparing to leave for the Academy, my mom told me I never needed her. She said she felt I thought she was stupid and useless. I was totally shocked. That was so far from the truth. I loved my mother and told her so. She explained she knew I loved her, but felt I found her generally useless beyond supplying my basic needs. I was so confused. I thought, *Isn't that the best kind of love, based solely on who you are, and not what you provide?* I realized I couldn't say that. I just hugged and kissed her and told her she was wrong.

I learned from this—being so blunt and literal could be hurtful to people. This was now an intrinsic part of who I was, and it would be difficult to change. Leaving home and

Hold Your Tongue

entering a world where I was surrounded by people making one inappropriate comment after another did nothing to improve my lack of tact. Although I tried to hold my tongue, this was very challenging at the Academy.

As shared in a previous reflection, the first words to my plebe summer company leadership—"Which one of you motherf*#kers wants to be next?"—strongly implies I still had much to learn about tact. Dealing with physical attacks and threats did not lend itself to tactful and courteous communication. Or, conversely, maybe I had not evolved enough to respond more gracefully. To be honest, I am *still* a work in progress under these conditions.

Some may think this behavior is totally understandable. Who would be gracious under those conditions? Would civility even be the appropriate tactic in terms of survival? The problem lies in providing too much information, unintentionally. Communication should be deliberate and purposeful. If someone said anything to offend me, I let them have it with both barrels. I didn't care who it was. I had to learn to be smarter than that. You never communicate your plan or lose control of your emotions while dealing with your adversary, no matter the provocation.

At the Academy, we had to memorize a 40-stanza poem, "The Laws of the Navy." The stanza I was required to repeat over and over again was, "Take heed what you say of your seniors, be your words spoken softly or plain, lest a bird of the air hear the matter, and so ye shall hear it again." (Does this sound similar to the scripture of my youth? Is

Hold Your Tongue

there a pattern here?)

Maybe if I had not shown my ability and willingness to physically fight, I wouldn't have had to do it so often. It became sport for some people. I was small, but I refused to back down to anybody. Potentially, things may not have progressed so quickly to other forms of warfare—like psychological and deprivation—had I been less assertive. A bird of the air was hearing the matter and adjusting the plan to be more effective. This was not an occasional occurrence. My mouth was getting me in trouble.

Again, on a particularly difficult day, Midshipman Titeasse' braced me up in the hall during our free time when we were supposed to be able to get a few moments of peace. That was very typical. Some Firsties behaved as though the MHP rule book did not exist. I was tired and absolutely furious! Midshipman Titeasse' was telling me how I didn't belong at *his* school and that the entire Brigade of Midshipmen would not rest until I left. I started to tremble uncontrollably, and a tear fell from my eye. His face was so close to mine, I could smell his putrid breath as his spittle landed on my face. A smile came across his face as he said, "Not so tough now, are you? Why are you crying? Have you had enough?" I responded—as required—with, "No excuse, sir."

Although plebes were required to only use the five basic responses, a Firstie could require a real answer. Midshipman Titeasse' did just that. Again, I never started it.

Hold Your Tongue

He said, "No really, I want to know why you're crying. Did I hurt your *f-e-e-lings*? Don't you want to go home?"

I guess he felt he had me on the ropes and he would continue until I threw in the towel. I looked directly in his face and answered his question: "Anyone this close to me is here either to ~~f*#k~~ ~~me~~ 'engage in meaningless sexual intercourse' or fight me. You will not do either. And if you don't get out of my face *right now*, I will kill you and spend the rest of my life in jail over a ~~piece of shit~~ 'misguided and troubled young man' like you. Sir." I meant every word of it and he knew it as he stepped back. We both glared at each other. Finally, he told me to get out of his sight.

The tactics changed after this. It seemed as though the word had gotten out that there was a need to take it to the next level with me. Seldom were the attacks one-on-one anymore. I was being approached by random midshipmen I didn't even know. Attacks also came while I was in in large anonymous groups, like being pushed down the stairs into King Hall or having rocks thrown at me from a distance as I walked to class. I had made them angry, and they were determined to teach me a lesson. Although it was a small portion of the Brigade that behaved this way, the silent majority gave tacit support.

I don't know if things would have been better if I had moderated my behavior. I knew my virulent tirades had definitely not improved my situation. My major issue was I spoke without having a plan. I didn't effectively use language to achieve my immediate objective. Additionally,

Hold Your Tongue

I had broken my angel mentor's rule and responded emotionally. Should I have held my tongue and tried to kill them with kindness, instead of just literally threatening to kill them? Or, was that type of assertiveness what was needed for the situation?

Over time, I did get smarter and remembered the lessons of my youth. *Would things have gotten better if I had remembered more quickly?* I wonder. I guess I'll never know. What I do know is that all communications should be deliberately delivered with specific intent. Being right is not enough. Wisdom is required in all communications. If you are incapable of communicating wisely—for any reason—hold your tongue.

The lessons of the mouthy little girl from Aiken, South Carolina were not lost on the midshipman I became. The challenge was to be strategic. I could be sweet and humble—or blunt and brash— but the decision of which path to choose needed to be a choice, not a knee jerk reaction. It was difficult, and to this day, I sometimes feel I must bite my tongue until it bleeds. But, I hold my tongue and pray for guidance — *No Coincidences.*

15 – Through the Pain

I loved martial arts. The poise and confidence it taught was invaluable. Having a great Sensei and Black Belt Team of instructors who taught character as well as combat helped to lay the foundation I needed in life. Our *dojo* was on a small side street right down the hill from the hospital. The Aiken Hospital was commissioned in 1917 by philanthropists Charles and Hope Iselin (part of the Winter Colony) and built by African-American contractors, McGhee and McGhee. Although the *dojo* seldom needed a hospital, it was convenient to have a medical facility close by.

Our *dojo* did not practice full contact karate. This meant when we were not using pads, we were to pull our punches and kicks, stopping about an inch away from the target and immediately retracting into the proper stance. If we fought in pads we could make light contact but never in the groin area. (Even with the best of intentions sometimes people still endured a solid hit.)

We were a competition *dojo*, so we met about three times a week and were also expected to practice at home. There was conditioning, combinations, sparring, and fundamentals almost every day. I was doing everything I could to qualify for the competition team. Our *dojo* did exceptionally well in *kumite* (sparring) and *kata* (detailed choreographed patterns of movements, or form). These were the two primary components of the competitions. We competed primarily in South Carolina, but also in Georgia—a very

Through the Pain

competitive region and the home of the Battle of Atlanta.

Established in 1970, the Battle of Atlanta—or simply, the Battle—was within its first few years of existence. Since its inception, the Battle has been staged 47 times over 46 years, to date. It has been home to some of the greatest fighters, forms and weapons competitors, and stars the martial arts world has ever known. From Chuck Norris to Evander Holyfield, Don Wilson, Bill "Superfoot" Wallace, Joe Lewis, Jeff Smith, and Jean-Claude Van Damme. Even back in the early- to mid-seventies, the Battle was a *huge* deal. I was determined to go.

Although I gender-integrated the *dojo*, it was otherwise very diverse. I learned to fight by sparring with men—most of whom were significantly larger than me—and I won most of the time. I practiced both *kata* and *kumite* every day for hours, and I watched the Senior Belts closely to learn from their techniques. My instructors were experienced competitors from the *dojo* in Georgia. They knew how to train winners. I was fortunate to have natural instincts and did well at executing the different combinations. Fighting came naturally to me.

I soon earned the opportunity to test for Yellow Belt. The belt progression was White, Yellow, Orange, Purple, Brown, and Black. It was my first experience at testing for a higher belt. If I was successful, I would no longer be an entry-level White Belt. I wanted to at least be a Yellow Belt if I qualified for the Battle. Testing was a serious event. The Sensei and other Black Belts instructed the students through various *kata* and combinations, appropriate for the belt-level sought. Even though I knew my moves, I was still really nervous.

A couple of other White Belts tested with me, and we performed each move on command, making corrections to techniques as dictated. Finally, the instructors surrounded me and watched intently. Although this was unnerving, I could tell they were impressed. But, they were unwilling to feed what they already saw as an over-inflated ego.

After a couple of minutes, the instructors walked in front of the testing students and—speaking in Japanese—brought us to attention. We were informed we all had passed. I was really excited because the other students had been training longer than I had. I made it! The next step was to gain approval to compete in the Battle.

One thing I knew, I would have to show I could control my temper during matches. I think my instructors felt I was ready from a technique perspective. I could spar far beyond my belt level and had spent many hours perfecting my *kata*. So, they began to test me. Since in the *dojo* we were not allowed to make contact without pads, they provided me with pads—and proceeded to summarily bounce me around the *dojo*.

It was so incredibly hard! Not just physically, but also from the perspective of maintaining control of my mind, tongue, and body. Losing control was not an option. If I lost control, I would get beaten. I had to focus on the art and everything

Through the Pain

I was taught to survive this test. These were large, young men and I didn't weigh 100 pounds soaking wet. One small lapse in judgement had already cost me a small cut to my lip. Somewhere in the middle of these bouts it was as though I just surrendered. I could only win their way. I could only win if I exercised control. It was a breakthrough moment, and everyone recognized it. I was going to the Battle.

The Battle of Atlanta was overwhelming! It was in a huge arena and there were over 1,000 *karatekas*—practitioners of karate—and thousands of avid karate fans. We arrived early for registration. There were teams from all over the country with colorful logos representing many different styles—our style was Zen Shotokai. The nation's premiere *karatekas* were in attendance. I was so excited to be there.

The format for the women was simpler than the format for the men. There were no weight classes for us—we fought until we lost. The first step was to win your belt, and then to fight the winners of the other belts until the final event. That night, the last woman standing from the lower belts would compete against the Black Belt Champion. All the greats were there. There were at least 15 rings going at any time when the competitions began. As the day continued, a crowd did start to form around the women's ring. One young teenage novice was cleaning the place up. Y'all, it was me!

I won the Yellow Belt division with ease. I then had to fight the winners of the other belts to determine my final

Through the Pain

standing. This occurred over the course of the entire day. The White and Yellow Belts may have been combined due to the low number of registrants and the justifiable unwillingness to tie up resources judging this event. After winning at this level, I progressed throughout the day winning against the Orange, Blue, Green, Purple, and Brown champions. I had qualified for the final event against the champion Black Belt woman to be televised that night. I had also overworked my left leg, which was swelling larger and larger every hour.

I had to wait several hours for the final event. My instructors kept asking if I wanted to forfeit and go to the hospital. I refused to leave. I had come this far, and I was not going to quit. By the time the match started, I was in excruciating pain. My left leg was swollen—including my knee—and I could barely stand on it. I still held my own. We swapped points back and forth until I basically could no longer move. The last two points were hers—she was the champion of the Battle of Atlanta.

My instructor immediately scooped me up, put me in a waiting car, and headed for the hospital. We were there for hours. The diagnosis was a severe sprain and bruising. I had to stay off my leg for a few weeks, but after that I was back at it. Most importantly, I did not quit. I finished what I started. I made it through the pain. I would need this kind of perseverance at the Academy.

At the Academy, I experienced an injury caused when an officer grabbed me from behind and slammed me to the floor. I never expected anything like that from this officer. The injury itself resulted in a misalignment of the patella. Simply put, my kneecap was out of place.

I never reported the initial injury. I would have had to be insane to do that. A "youngster"—sophomore—who ruins the career of an Academy graduate would have no chance of survival. And women were already struggling for acceptance. My reporting him would have been a major stumbling block for all women. If I went to medical, they would have asked how it happened and I couldn't lie—so I didn't seek treatment. Had I gone to medical, I would have been excused from physical training until it had an opportunity to heal. Not being a doctor, I'm not sure if it would have healed on its own.

Fortunately we had a short break from school and my knee felt better. After returning from the break gymnastics training commenced. When I stuck my landing, my knee gave way. It felt like the original injury—when I was lifted in the air and brought down so fast and so hard I had no time to plant my foot. During gymnastics I landed on the side of my foot and my knee popped. I will never forget the pain. After this second injury, I was taken straight to medical and I could answer honestly—it happened after I jumped off the gymnastics bars.

With minimal physical therapy and no attempt at a basic patella realignment procedure, I was told I was to receive a more complex knee surgery. The relatively new Elmslie-Trillat procedure was performed. This technique was being

Through the Pain

studied by the surgeon who later wrote several papers on the topic. I was left with a seven-inch scar, a screw in my tibia that produced constant pain, and a knee locked straight with no ability to bend. I was told that as "government property," I had no say regarding this surgery. My only option was to quit. I was not going to do that.

I heard the term "government property" mostly from medical personnel, and I hated being called it almost as much as "nigger." It seemed to strip me of all my rights as a human being. If I injured myself, I was told I could be charged with Destruction of Government Property. I didn't know if all this was true. *Who was I going to ask?* If I learned nothing else from my experiences at the Academy, I learned not to make my problems someone else's. I had Invisible Friends. We would just need to make it through the pain.

After removing the straight leg cast—and informing me the cast should have been bent—the physician turned me over to physical therapy to try to bend the knee. This was absolute torture. The screw site hurt all the time and the pain left me with a very noticeable limp, still walking with my foot turned inward. The therapy sessions were spent with people trying to forcibly bend my knee that had healed straight and locked. It is painful even today to recall these experiences. The medical staff finally decided to perform a manipulation under anesthesia. I asked what that meant, and was told I would be put to sleep and the knee would be snapped to achieve full range of motion. No one seemed to know what the outcome of this procedure would be. They just said the procedure would be done—and we would see what happened.

Now put yourself in my shoes. There was no kind, bedside manner or real explanation of what was being done to me throughout this process. All I felt was, *I'm in this hostile environment, surrounded by people who don't want me here.* The keys to my survival had been my strong moral upbringing, my intellect, and my physical abilities. One third of my skills were seriously compromised, and I was terrified. I knew that with one bad leg I could still probably hold my own against a single adversary, but multiple combatants would pose a real problem. My reactions could not be as deliberate and controlled. This kind of fear did not bode well for anyone. My threats to kill people who physically threatened me—well, their threats might now actually occur due to my diminished ability to control my defenses. I was like a cornered animal—I felt under attack from every direction. On top of all this, my leg *really* hurt—every day, all day.

So, they did it. I was taken to Hospital Point, put to sleep, and they snapped my knee. At least that's what I was told had occurred. When I awakened, and the anesthesia and pain medicines wore off, the pain was horrible. The medical staff got me up on crutches as soon as possible. As I remember it, my leg was wrapped in something that resembled a soft cast or elaborate brace. I continued to walk with a limp, my knee turned inward when I tried to bend it, so stairs were a problem and that screw continued to be a source of constant pain. This injury plagued me for my last

Through the Pain

three years at the Academy.

Why didn't I just quit? I could have left and gone to see doctors who I believed had my best interest at heart. Who stays in a place under these circumstances? Excellent questions! I never really considered leaving. I made a promise to a bent and wrinkled old woman on an Annapolis side-street—and I intended to see it through. They could kill me—and there were times I thought that might happen—but I would *not* quit. I can't explain why I never processed what was happening to me in its totality. I only focused on surviving the next minute. I never dwelled on any of it. I just needed to be ready for the next challenge.

My knee issues didn't exempt me from the physical requirements for graduation. I still had to run a mile in at least seven minutes and thirty seconds. I had to swim for 40 minutes and perform all kinds of lifesaving activities and timed stroke drills—freestyle, breaststroke, backstroke, sidestroke. I managed to get through most of them by the skin of my teeth. There were definitely no world records being broken. I spent a lot of time in the pool. I preferred the cool water to the pounding track. That's why the last mile run that stood between me and graduation was so traumatic.

I still walked with a crooked limp and each step was painful. I didn't know how I was going to pass this mile, but I had to try. Seven minutes and thirty seconds should have been plenty of time under normal conditions—but I was not experiencing normal conditions. Several midshipmen were

Through the Pain

in Halsey Field House that afternoon. I was not the only one whose testing was delayed due to physical issues. The key word is delayed—not waived. We *had* to pass these tests. When they told everyone else to run—but told me to wait—I got nervous. I remembered what happened to me the last time I was told to run alone after my neck injury. I tried to be positive and accept the explanation that they didn't want me to get in the way of the other runners. That actually made sense. There would be nothing graceful about this attempt to pass the mile run.

My concern increased after everyone else completed the run, and I was not instructed to begin until they all left the field house. This was too eerily familiar. I wasn't sure what to expect when they called me to the track. I was so relieved when they told me to get ready to run, reminding me I had to finish in less than seven minutes and thirty seconds. I was being timed by two young men. I didn't know who they were, but I assumed they were part of the Academy's Physical Education Department.

One of the men said, "Get ready. Get set. Go!" No one was in the field house but the three of us, and I was very awkwardly half-running and swinging my stiff leg along as fast as I could. To my surprise and delight, they started cheering for me. The pain was intense, not only in my leg but also my hips and lower back. I had to make four laps around the track. They kept yelling my time to me and telling me when I needed to speed up. Running was taking everything I had, but I had to try. I had to give it my all.

At the end of the third lap, one of the young men said I was

Through the Pain

on pace and I could make it. I just had to keep going. This was much easier said than done. By now every muscle in my body was screaming. The only screaming that was comparable was the encouragement of the two young men. When I rounded the corner of the last lap, they said, "Run!" And I did. I probably looked like some sort of large earthbound prehistoric bird being chased by a saber tooth tiger. But I ran. They were screaming out my time as I neared the finish line. As I crossed, they happily cheered, "Seven, twenty-seven!" I passed the mile with three seconds to spare.

I collapsed on the track, crying and just trying to catch my breath. I think the tears surprised them. They kept saying, "You passed!" I didn't have the energy to make them understand my tears were a combination of joy and pain. I only had enough lung capacity to say, "Thank you." They smiled and asked if I was okay before they left. I assured them I was, and that I would be leaving soon. *I fought the good fight,* I thought. *I finished the race. I kept the faith.* I was happy. I made it through the pain — *No Coincidences.*

16 – A Few Good Friends

"Friend" is a term that I rarely use. I have always tried to be good to everyone and to be helpful. This left me with many acquaintances. For me, a friend is someone with whom I have a symbiotic relationship based on our mutual well-being. There were very few of these people when I was growing up. My independent nature made it difficult for anyone to breach that wall. But, there was one little girl I will never forget.

Kelley was a beautiful little girl with exceptionally long, wavy blond hair and the brightest blue eyes. She was also really smart and in the gifted program, too. I will never forget the day she was introduced to our class as having just moved to town. She wore obviously used, oversized clothing and well-worn shoes. I noticed the assessing eyes of my privileged classmates and even heard snickering from some of the girls. She had been judged, found unacceptable, and summarily dismissed—all in about two minutes. What was amazing about her was she either didn't notice or didn't care. A girl after my own heart, she had the biggest brightest smile on her face. It was at that very moment I decided to do whatever I could to keep that smile on her face.

After her introduction, class continued as usual. She sat in an empty chair near the back of the room. I glanced back at her as the teacher provided instructions regarding the class work. She was obviously lost as she tried to determine what materials the teacher was referencing, and no one offered to assist. As soon as the class ended, I made a beeline to her

A Few Good Friends

and offered to show her to the next class. We all went to the same classes, but she didn't know and no one else offered to escort her. As we walked to class, I introduced myself and welcomed her to school. I told her about the classes and, with few exceptions, we all took the same courses. I looked at her schedule and it was identical to mine. My classmates looked at me, quizzically and with a mildly disapproving demeanor. I didn't care. I was going to be nice to her—and they were, too—whether they liked it or not.

Kelley sat next to me in all my classes and we became best friends. She had one of the purest souls I have ever met. She never made negative comments about people and generally maintained a very positive attitude about everything. Despite the fact her family faced financial challenges and she was surrounded by very privileged children, she never complained or compared her situation to others. I still maintained my relationships with the other students, but our activities now also included Kelley. Although I could tell the other kids were uncomfortable with her appearance, they had to admit she was really nice and also very intelligent.

Kelley's father was a junior enlisted man in the Air Force. He was stationed at the Aiken Air Force Station, a Cold War U.S. Air Force Radar Station located about 6.4 miles northeast of town—not far from where I lived. The base operated a SAGE—Semi-Automatic Ground Environment—System, a U.S. Air Defense System designed to protect the United States against nuclear attack by Soviet bombers. I always thought it was there to protect

A Few Good Friends

the Savannah River Site nuclear weapons facility.

Junior enlisted men received very little pay. Based on their income, most qualified for public assistance. This was obviously true of Kelley's father. She wore the same things over and over again, but her clothing was always clean and pressed. We were about the same size, so I started bringing her clothes and shoes to wear. I was by no means as privileged as my classmates, but we were comfortable. We were not so comfortable that my mom didn't notice the missing clothes. When I told her what I was doing, she was initially perturbed. But when I explained the situation, she understood. She said I could rotate clothing with Kelley, but she needed to send it back and my mom would take care of cleaning. We would mix and match the pieces so it wasn't obvious to others. And my mom could make clothing quickly and expertly. Between the three of us, it was our secret.

We were inseparable and always had each other's backs. I don't think Kelley's family was initially comfortable with the relationship—we never visited each other's homes. Kelley only lived in Aiken about two years. In the second year, she was able to convince her parents to let her visit me in my home. She soon was spending the night on the weekends, then spending several nights, and finally she seldom went home except over the weekend. I never met her parents. They would drop her off and pick her up without ever getting out of the car. I didn't care. I was just happy Kelley was there.

A Few Good Friends

When I think of how my parents just accepted this without question, it reinforced my belief they were exceptionally good people. They had one more child to feed and clothe, and they did so without complaint. She was a nice girl and soon became part of the family.

Kelley and I were social with our other classmates, but I sacrificed some "cool" points by befriending her. I didn't care. I had a few good friends, but Kelley was number one. I knew many of the other students in my class, and I participated in enough activities to be fairly well regarded by the crowd, but I suffered from no illusions they would ever be as loyal as Kelley. My parents were fairly well-known and respected, so that bought me social credibility. But credibility based on status and material things can be as fleeting as the kind of friends it engenders. We had no need to worry about our "friends" making cruel comments behind our backs or acting in ways detrimental, demeaning, or disloyal. We were each other's friend and only encouraged and supported one another. That kind of friendship is almost impossible to achieve when you depend on a crowd.

The day Kelley's dad was transferred was one of the saddest days I can remember. The base actually closed in 1975, but Kelley was gone by then. Due to my lack of responsiveness, I lost contact with her. For years, she sent Christmas cards, even after I went to the Academy. I never responded. I took our friendship for granted. I thought she would always stay in touch and after I graduated I would go and see her. When the cards stopped, initially I didn't notice. When I did, it

A Few Good Friends

was too late. I couldn't find her. She deserved better than that, and I'm ashamed I didn't maintain our relationship. She will always be loved. She was a dear friend and I learned to be a better friend based on losing Kelley. Again, of my few good friends, she was the best.

Making friends at the Academy was a challenge for me. Again, I had many acquaintances, but no true friends. A few of the upperclass black males were kind and included all of us plebes in their activities. I had a couple of really great guys in my company, but I was careful not to make them "collateral damage" by sharing my challenges with them. I'm certain they would have been appalled and ridden in on their "white horses" to save me. That response would have been at their own peril. That was not supposition. Remember, I was given this warning.

As mentioned, black male midshipmen faced their own set of challenges. Due to the negative attention related to their friendships with "MidshipChicks," many steered clear. This was especially true of my black male classmates. Having said that, I did have one special friend. I'm not sure he ever knew how important he was to me. We met under less than optimal conditions, and it was this one particular experience that endeared him to me.

He was a big football player who was very loud and could be equally as intimidating. Since he was a football player, I rarely came in contact with him. This all changed one Saturday afternoon when football season was over. Upperclassmen could grant us permission to come into their

A Few Good Friends

rooms while they were gone and listen to music. A black male first class football player gave me this privilege. Plebes were not allowed to listen to music, and I desperately missed the soulful rhythms of my culture.

I kept checking to see if they were gone, and when I found the room empty I was overcome with excitement at the prospect of playing records on his very elaborate stereo system. I listened to the Spinners, Lou Rawls, Marilyn McCoo, and the indomitable Aretha. I was so engrossed in the music, I didn't initially notice the large black plebe standing in the door.

He said with absolute authority he was there to listen to music. I told him I was given permission by the upperclassman from my company to use his system and he could come back later. He was obviously very dissatisfied with this response and used his considerable size to tower over me, telling me to get lost. It was obvious this was a regular privilege he enjoyed, and he considered me to be an inconvenient interloper. Well, I had waited for this opportunity and no one was going to chase me away. I only had a short period of time before the Firsties returned. So, I looked up at him and provided specific directions to Hades while continuing to play the music.

I could tell he was shocked by this shrimp of a woman who dared to speak to him this way, even after he had towered over her with his best grizzly bear imitation. So, he decided to take the direct approach. He walked over to the stereo, took the album off I was listening to, and put on the music

A Few Good Friends

he had brought with him. Feeling satisfied he had made his point, he ignored me as he sat down comfortably to enjoy his tunes. When I started to move, I felt his eyes glaring at me. I walked to the stereo, removed his album, and returned the music I was enjoying to the turntable. He looked at me with a combination of disbelief and aggravation as he again switched the albums.

Well, he was not the only one exasperated with the situation. This time, he didn't sit down, but instead stood next to the stereo, looking at me with eyes that dared me to move. I got up, walked to the stereo as he looked down at me. I quickly snatched his album off the turntable, scratching it with the needle. I held it up and said, "Now play this!" as I snapped it across my knee. From the look on his face, I knew I was in trouble. He picked me up and tossed me over to the bed, commanding me not to move.

I just sat there glaring at him until I heard the Firsties returning. And then I started to cry. He looked at me in absolute horror and ran over towards me, stood in front of me, and begged me to stop crying. That is where my Firstie found him—looming over me as I sat on the bed crying uncontrollably. My Firstie was furious as he yelled at him, asking what was going on. Before he could answer, through my sobs, I pointed up at him and said, "He hit me." My classmate could not get any words out before he found himself on the floor getting the crap beat out of him. I slowly got up to leave, wiping my eyes, and was reassured by my Firstie he would not bother me again. When I was sure no one was looking, my eyes briefly connected with my subdued classmate, and I gave him a taunting smile as I walked out of the room. From that point on we were besties.

I don't know why he befriended me. Maybe because he thought I was crazy and in need of a keeper. What I came to realize was that when I was with him, no one bothered me. I cannot explain how good that feeling was. Imagine being on alert all the time, just waiting for the next attack. Now I was able to relax. I had almost forgotten how to do that. It only lasted as long as I was with him, but it was wonderful. He probably wondered why I followed him around like a puppy. We argued all the time, and never had a kind word to say to each other. But, he still tolerated my presence. I'm not sure he knew it, but he was my brother. He was my friend. I could be moody, snippy, and downright rude, and he would just look at me like I was crazy. Did I mention he always started it?

We both dated other people—that was not the nature of our relationship. He had quite a few friends among the black males of our class. I think he was fairly popular in general—I don't know why. He could be such a jerk. Maybe he saved that "charming" part of his personality just for me. I, on the other hand, was friendly but had very few friends (according to my narrow definition of friend). But I could always depend on him.

My father said people only needed a few good friends. He said being a part of the crowd was a sure path to destruction. Continuing from his favorite scriptures in the seventh chapter of the book of Matthew: "But small is the gate and

A Few Good Friends

narrow the road that leads to life, and only a few find it."

You only need a few good friends. Lead—do not follow the crowd. At the Academy, I had few bonds of friendship. But that was all I needed. I remain eternally grateful for my friends. The lesson I learned with Kelley years before laid the foundation for a friendship with my classmate that has lasted until this day — *No Coincidences*.

17 – "When People Show You Who They Are..."

"When people show you who they are, believe them."
– Maya Angelou

I always wanted to see the best in people and didn't believe some were just bad to the core. This tendency left me vulnerable to people who meant to do me harm.

When we get older, we have the opportunity to look back on ourselves from the perspective of age and experience. I think I was a young piece of work. As is true with most teenagers, I thought I knew everything and was predisposed to share my opinion. As mentioned in other reflections, I did not usually proactively share my thoughts, but if asked or if included in a discussion, I had the answer. To add insult to injury, the combination of my faith and confidence left me with a fairly black and white, intolerant perspective on most topics. It was either right or wrong and there was absolutely one correct way to address the issue.

From my protected, well-taken care of world, I had no concept of the challenges other youths faced. Also, I had the benefit of parents who were constantly educating me regarding what was expected of a good, contributing member of society. I didn't realize at the time this was the exception rather than the rule, and other kids probably found me "preachy" and judgmental when they brought up things that were happening in their lives. What was likely further exacerbating about me was that 95% of the time, I

When People Show You Who They Are...

was right. Exactly what I told them would happen, happened. This was not a tribute to my intellect, but to the constant tutelage of my parents and the guidance of my Invisible Friends.

I believe communication is 25% message and 75% delivery. It didn't matter that I was right. If I delivered the message in a judgmental, self-righteous tone—people couldn't hear what I was saying because they couldn't get past how I was saying it. My attempts to help were probably agitating to some and precipitated more than a few behind-the-back eye rolls. I think my tone was so forceful and decisive, other kids felt uncomfortable telling me I didn't understand or that their issue was more complicated than my solution. Or maybe, that wasn't the case at all. I believe they may have agreed my response was appropriate, but couldn't understand how to execute the idea. I learned over the years that solutions or opportunities without pathways to achieving them are only illusively frustrating images of the unattainable.

I say all this to help in understanding why some kids might have been turned off by me. They either had to be very self-confident and/or understanding. I was actually a very good and loyal friend. I didn't abandon people because they made a mistake or became unpopular. I would give people the shirt off my back and wouldn't say anything behind the back I wouldn't say face to face. This group of tolerant people would either just ignore the delivery of my message because they knew it was meant in love, ignore me, or tell me they didn't like the way I said it. Either way was fine

When People Show You Who They Are...

with me, but I preferred the latter. The correction helped me to grow.

Contrastingly, there were people I befriended who became envious, were determined to shake my confidence, and/or just walked away from the relationship. This was particularly true of a girl who moved to our town named Fannie. No one paid any attention to her. This can be expected in a small town where relationships are built from the crib and it's difficult for an outsider to penetrate these groups. Additionally, her appearance was different than most of the other kids. But I approached her, introduced myself, and tried to make her feel comfortable in her new surroundings. I had a real attraction to the underdog. Again, I think this was due to my parent's influence. I didn't like to see people suffer if I could be of assistance.

Fannie and I became friends. She was both nice and smart. We visited one another's homes and generally enjoyed each other's company. As we grew older, parties, dating, and relationships with boys all became part of what was required to be "popular." All of these were prohibited in my parents' house. Boys couldn't call until I was fifteen, and I couldn't go out socially with boys until I was sixteen. So, the drinking, drugs, and sex of teenage life were not part of my plan. And, as was my character, I had no hesitancy in explaining why. This produced an ever-widening rift between me and my friend Fannie.

Fannie and I were acquainted with a group of girls who were popular, attractive, athletic, intelligent (though not gifted), and who were all moving through the phases of finding themselves. They were experimenting with different things and had much more liberty to hang out and do as they pleased than I did. I guess I didn't notice when we started to go in different directions until the division was well underway. (I could be clueless like that. I didn't need my friends to be like me.) I might comment on behaviors I saw as self-destructive, but I still considered them my friends. Finally, I did notice Fannie had started to pull away in favor of a group of "popular girls." She seemed drawn to their activities and enjoyed the new experiences.

The time we spent together at lunch ceased. We no longer sat next to each other in the few classes we shared, and the weekend visits came to a halt. Fannie had new friends, a boyfriend, and was getting involved in athletics and the active teenage social life. Even though we no longer spent time together, I still didn't get the message and continued to consider her a friend. I was so busy with academics, clubs, student government, community activities, martial arts, and everything else thrown my way that I really didn't dwell on it. Fannie seemed happy, so I was happy for her. While being happy, I was also concerned about the rumors I was hearing regarding the choices she was making. Her new best friends were the same girls who had been mocking her behind her back the year before. I was afraid they would eventually hurt her, but I could tell she wasn't interested in what I thought. Fannie barely spoke to me, yet I remained loyal. I guess I was slow to recognize the total collapse of the friendship because I didn't want to, and I was so busy. She was showing me who she was, and I wasn't paying

When People Show You Who They Are…

attention.

One day at school, Fannie and her new friends decided enough was enough and they needed to onboard me or sever the relationship. My friend approached me with several other girls and told me either I would start to do the cool things they were doing and accept their lifestyle as my own, or I could no longer be their friend. I never considered most of them friends anyway. They were at best cordial acquaintances, but Fannie was my friend. I had always been nice to her even when no one else had given her a chance and yet here she stood with these girls echoing their sentiment. Fannie and her friends were giving me an ultimatum in a very smug, take-it-or-leave-it fashion.

I left it. I laughed at them and told them if those were the conditions for their friendship and what was required to be "popular," then I chose to pass on the opportunity. It probably would have been more gracious if I had left it there, but I added the prophecy that I would see all of them pregnant before we graduated from high school—and I would laugh in their faces. (I know, not nice, but I said it.) You might think there would have been loud protests or name calling, but I think they were shocked at my response. Maybe they had done that to Fannie and other members of the group and everyone had acquiesced to their terms. Maybe they knew I was not someone to be played with, and if they wanted to maintain their beautifully aligned dental work, they needed to step back. For whatever reason, they walked away and that was that.

When People Show You Who They Are...

I never had any real relationship with Fannie after that. My prophecy for most of those girls came true—although most made it go away privately. I'm sure I was the butt of their jokes, but she who laughs last, laughs best. I remained popular with the student body, won awards, had fun, dated, and achieved all my goals. Although Fannie's behavior was hurtful, I should have seen it coming and been emotionally prepared. I just didn't want to believe it. When people show you who they are, believe them. My endless optimism made this concept difficult for me, and I faced this challenge again at the Academy.

I entered the Academy with great expectations—even though I had been warned via an unwelcoming call that I would be the only black woman in the first class of women. If I had done my research, I would have found this was the pattern for the first black men to be admitted to the Academy. Come in alone; leave. But I—with my eternal optimism—didn't focus on this. I was very accustomed to being the only black and/or female in an organization or group and the challenges accompanying this condition. Having these experiences in my past was not a coincidence. Neither was learning that people usually show you who they are. You just have to believe them.

In addition to being accustomed to being the "only," I was very comfortable with having white friends. I didn't think of finding a female friend as being an obstacle. Eighty-one girls were admitted in this inaugural class. Surely, I would find one or two good friends. Remember, I believe in having only "a few good friends." I underestimated the

When People Show You Who They Are...

intensity of the feelings regarding the admission of women to the Academy. Many of the same individuals who were against women felt the same way about black people. What I was to experience at the Academy made growing up in a small, southern town seem like child's play. This included experiencing very distant relationships with the women.

I was not the exception as it related to relationships with other women. Few of we Academy women formed strong friendships outside of our immediate surroundings. We were not allowed to meet as a group to support one another. That was considered a "mutiny." Most women decided to move into their own personal survival mode. There were small groups of two or three that formed friendships. Roommates or people from similar backgrounds also spent time together to provide mutual support. The greatest opportunity for comradery was among sports teams. But there was no underground effort to form a support group for women—no Eighth Battalion.

With the injury to my knee, my opportunity to form friendships through sports was short lived. I tried to form relationships with some of the girls in my company but I never dwelled on this too much. I had much bigger fish to fry and couldn't afford to be disillusioned by whether someone liked me or not. I would have liked to have had female friends, but that wasn't in the cards for me. I often wonder if Alicia had anything to do with this.

When I initially met Alicia, I thought she was nice. She acted as though she wanted to be my friend. It didn't take long for me to start questioning who she really was when I heard her spew vitriolic comments regarding a group of people. I should have known then that if she could be so hateful toward that group, her venomous feelings for me would eventually manifest themselves. Remember the concept of contagion? I asked her why she felt the way she did about the group, and she had no good reason. Is there ever a good reason for lumping people together in a group and hating them? I told her I didn't think this was right—she said I didn't understand.

Alicia seemed to want to be my friend, and I think this deception caused me to fail to notice little comments and acts of jealousy. Many women did whatever it took to gain the favor of the men. They were focused on fitting in and being accepted. Understandably, they tried to avoid being the butt of cruel jokes and harassment. Alicia was no exception to this rule. Combining this need with her proven ability to justify group hate should have been enough to put me on alert. I just didn't want to believe it. I had always been nice to her.

There were several other women I started to form relationships with, but each friendship ended abruptly with no explanation. When I asked if I had done something to offend them, I never got a response. The friendships just ended. It reminded me of my friendship with Fannie. I could still be pretty direct and intolerant of inane comments, so I thought maybe that was the reason. Even when I made a point of biting my tongue during these instances, the friendships still didn't last long. Alicia was always in the

When People Show You Who They Are...

shadows—close by and listening. I attributed this to her trying to be my friend. I ignored all the warning signs.

Whether it was in support of the Academy efforts to get rid of me, or an expression of her personal objections to me, or just her being who she was, Alicia decided to be my enemy. Any time she saw me forming relationships, she would work to destroy them. What was interesting is she convinced my new friends that if they talked to me about whatever infraction she was accusing me of, I would know it was her and she would be in danger. She told people I said hateful things about them, that I was a racist, a slut, disloyal, and that I was using them to further some personal agenda. She told anyone I was getting close to that I didn't really care about them as a friend.

How did she pull this off? She was always around. She knew me well enough to be able to mimic words or phrases to make it sound like me. She observed the relationships enough to pick up pieces of information she could distort and blame it on me. She even placed a veiled racial insult in a publication. While I eventually learned to feed her with a long-handled spoon, I still didn't understand how detrimental she was. She had people fooled. She was very good at what she did. Sweet, innocent Alicia meant nothing good for me.

It took years for people to start to come to me and tell me what was going on. After I read the comment in the publication, I knew it was true. Alicia showed me who she was the first day I met her when she released the hateful

When People Show You Who They Are…

tirade against a particular group of people. I wonder how many wonderful friendships I was deprived of by Alicia.

Just as I had done with Fannie, I tried to ignore the warning signs. But unlike Fannie, I never let her get close enough to emotionally hurt me by her betrayal. She had shown me who she was and based on my previous experience with Fannie, I never really trusted her. Fannie was no coincidence, and although I was reluctant to accept Alicia would do me harm, at least I never let her into my heart.

At the Academy, my trusting naivety took me on a tumultuous rollercoaster ride. I finally came to understand I couldn't make excuses for everyone. Even a woman I thought was my friend was working behind the scenes to get rid of me. Some people were exactly what they seemed. I continue to believe these people are a small minority, but they do exist, and from time to time, we encounter these snakes.

"I saved you," cried that woman
"And you've bit me even, why?
And you know your bite is poisonous and now I'm gonna die."
"Oh shut up, silly woman," said the reptile with a grin,
"You knew damn well I was a snake before you brought me in."
(Excerpt from "The Snake" by Al Wilson)

When people show you who they are, believe them — *No Coincidences.*

18 – Warrior Up

In this book of reflections, I share very personal experiences of injustice, disappointment, and victory. My goal is not to evoke pity for myself as a poor victim. I have been many things in my life, but a "victim" is not one of them. The experiences of my youth occurred due to paths I intentionally chose. The poet Robert Frost summarizes this concept in the last stanza of one of my favorite poems, "The Road Not Taken":

> *I shall be telling this with a sigh*
> *Somewhere ages and ages hence:*
> *Two roads diverged in a wood, and I—*
> *I took the one less traveled by,*
> *And that has made all the difference.*

My father also often preached that the road to destruction is occupied by a great crowd of people, but the road to salvation is a lonely one. As a child, I chose to be different. I chose difficult courses. I chose to lead organizations that had never been led by someone who looked like me. I chose to stand up for the underdog and tried to do what was right, even if it was unpopular. I also chose to do some really dumb stuff. And just as we all will, I faced the consequences for all these choices, both good and bad. I never relinquished the responsibility for what happened in my life to others—no matter how culpable they were for my situation. That would give them a power they didn't deserve, or—more accurately—even possess.

Warrior Up

I quickly learned even the "good" decisions often had a perilous pathway I had to first travel before I reaped the benefits. Isn't it interesting how the bad decisions seemed to have just the opposite effect? Bad decisions often resulted in relatively instantaneous gratification that placed me on a downhill pathway to negative consequences.

I knew all this—at least conceptually—when I chose to walk into a largely all-male Naval Junior Reserve Officer Training Corps (NJROTC) program. The NJROTC unit was housed in a large white trailer behind the single-storied brick buildings that made up Schofield Junior High School. Schofield housed the ninth and tenth grades. I chose this with full anticipation of leadership and commitment. With a Marine Gunnery Sergeant as the unit instructor, we were a very professional unit. I don't remember if I was the only black female or the only female, period. I seldom noticed those things. Someone else always made a big deal of it.

As you might imagine, the NJROTC kids were not considered to be part of the "in-crowd," but we not labeled as misfits either. We were members of the student council, class officers, athletes, and club leaders. Most importantly, we were being trained to serve in the military with all the responsibilities that entails. In addition to naval history, ships, planes, submarines, and armament, we also learned the expectations of honor and proper deportment. As if it were not enough that my parents expected exemplary behavior because I represented God, them, and myself—the sergeant was telling me that by choosing to put on this uniform, I chose to represent my nation.

Warrior Up

That was a lot of responsibility for a 15-year-old girl who, in addition to seeking scholarship opportunities, was just experiencing the increased freedom of a high school student. My peers were experimenting with alcohol, sex, and drugs. They seemed to have it all under control because the adults still saw them as outstanding young pillars of society. *Yeah, right!*

It was with all these competing conditions in mind I was faced with another choice. There was going to be a house party, with no adults at home. Everyone was talking about it, and an older boy I thought was *really* cute asked me if I was going. He was handsome, tall, and athletic, but he was kind of a bad boy—the kind proper young girls like me were often attracted to. I said I was going. I was trying to be cool even though I knew my parents would very likely say no. I also knew "the Sarge" would not approve, but I heard I wouldn't be the only NJROTC cadet in attendance.

That Friday evening, I came home, cleaned the house, showed my parents a stack of tests and homework graded with all As. I told them about all the responsible activities I was performing at school, and they told me this was all good. Then I sprung the question on them: "Do you think I can go to a party with my friends tonight?" Next began the grand inquisition. They wanted to know who I was going with, where I was going, would adults be there, would there be drinking or drugs, did they know the family…? I knew better than to lie to my parents, so I answered evasively, focusing on my level of responsibility and arguing they would not always be there to make decisions for me. I told them they should trust me, and I needed to start to learn for myself.

It sounded good to me, but they were not having it. "We won't always be there, but we're here now," was my answer. "And it's our responsibility to protect you from bad situations. It's not you that we don't trust. But the entire situation could go bad very quickly." They were not much for explanations. I was raised in a "because I said so!" household. As you might imagine, my teenage brain found this decision to be undeserved and dictatorial. I decided I would show them and go anyway.

In an earlier reflection, I mentioned we didn't live right on the street but down a dirt and gravel road. It would be easy to sneak out the back door off the den, walk to the main road, and catch a ride to the party. I had it all figured out. I would go to the party and be back long before my parents would notice I was gone.

We went to bed pretty early in my household, so when I got up at 11:00 p.m. to quickly put on my coolest outfit, everyone else was fast asleep. The boy would be at the top of the driveway to pick me up at 11:30. He said if I wasn't there, he wouldn't wait. My father had a reputation regarding protecting the well-being of his daughters. No sane young man wanted to run into my dad while hanging around his property late at night. As I dressed, all my parents' warnings were running through my mind. But I was intimately familiar with all the doom and gloom predictions for a disobedient girl. Interestingly enough, the

Warrior Up

voice I heard in my head more loudly was the Sergeant. You see, I loved my parents, but I didn't choose them. I *did* choose NJROTC, and I promised to behave in a certain manner. I could be dismissed from the unit—or at least demoted—if I were caught at this kind of party. Even worse, the Sarge would be very disappointed.

All these thoughts were running through my mind as I stood in my yard, all cute and made up with my skirt rolled up around my waist to achieve a length that left little to the imagination. I saw the car lights as they stopped at the end of the road. I started to walk toward the road, but then stopped cold. I couldn't do it. I had made a choice, and this choice came with certain responsibilities. He sat there waiting longer than I expected and to my horror, I watched as the lights turned into the road. Fortunately, he was just turning in to turn around. I turned to go back inside to go to bed when I saw my father looking out his bedroom window. Neither of us said anything. I just went back inside and went to bed. He never mentioned the incident to me.

The party didn't go well. The police raided the party and several kids were actually arrested for drugs. I was told the handsome young man would have been a father nine months later if the girl had not made the decision to terminate her pregnancy. I can imagine that decision haunted her for the rest of her life.

So, why did I decide not to go? I had to "warrior up." Being a warrior is not just about what I did as a cadet and person, but what I did not do. I made a choice—a commitment to a certain kind of life. If I was to ever be the kind of officer the sergeant was training me to be, it was to be a 24/7 commitment. I reaped the benefits and complied with the restrictions because, bottom line, the choice was mine. If I was not up to the task, I needed to make a different choice. I wasn't going to quit NJROTC. I would also have to "warrior up" many times during my four years at the Academy.

When the Academy admitted women in 1976, by law, women were not allowed to serve in combat. There were numerous debates as to whether women should be admitted without changing this restriction. But, in October 1975, President Gerald Ford signed Public Law 94-106 which included a mandate stating the United States' military academies were to begin admitting women in the fall of 1976. He signed the military authorization bill with a rider including the statement:

> *"...the secretaries of the military departments concerned shall take such action as may be necessary and appropriate to insure that (1) female individuals shall be eligible for appointment and admission to the service academy concerned, beginning with appointment to such academy for the class beginning in the calendar year 1976, and (2) the academic and other relevant standards required for appointment, admissions, training, graduation, commissioning of female individuals shall be the same as those*

> *required for male individuals, except for those minimum essential adjustments in such standards required because of physiological differences between male and female individuals."*

It was determined the admission of women would not change the academy's mission of training midshipmen to be professional officers in the naval service. However, women midshipmen would not be able to use their combat training because of the wording of U. S. Code Title 10:

> *"...women may not be assigned to duty in aircraft that are engaged in combat missions nor can they be assigned to duty on vessels of the Navy other than hospital ships and transports."*

As you might imagine, there was much wringing of hands and gnashing of teeth regarding the conundrum of training noncombatants in a combat school. This is not a debate I intend to engage in here. Merriam-Webster defines the word "warrior" as a person engaged or experienced in warfare. This definition does not distinguish between, race, gender, religion, or any of the demographical categories we use to define ourselves.

My choice to attend the Academy was a difficult one for me. Members of my family had served in the Army and Marine Corps, so military service was not foreign to me. I held those family members in the highest esteem, but I never really saw myself as following in their footsteps. I had the world available to me. As mentioned in a previous reflection, I was accepted to every Ivy League school to which I applied, and I even had an ROTC scholarship. Why would I give all that up for the Academy?

The Academy is what I had been prepared to do. This was part of the plan for me, if I chose to accept it. It explained why I had always been the only black and/or female; why I had selected such a strong STEM curriculum; why opportunities were stolen, and grades were changed; why I learned to fight men and was a warrior by nature; and why I was born to my parents at this place and time. None of it was a coincidence. This challenge was mine to face. It was my choice.

Was I excited about it? No. But I understood the nature of the commitment I was making. I hoped Harvard and MIT were still in my future, but the immediate task was the United States Naval Academy. I had no idea how difficult this task would be. Had I known, I probably would have still done it. But, I would not have been so disappointed by the behaviors of people I previously held in such high esteem. That part was difficult.

So, I arrived at the Academy prepared to become a professional naval officer—to be a warrior. I must admit, I received that preparation in spades. I would often attempt to ease my concerns about the way I was being treated with the realization that if I went to war, I needed to be prepared to face all of that and more. I sometimes wondered if this was what war felt like. Although there were times I actually did fear for my life, I knew combat was worse.

This rationalization did little to make me feel better when I experienced the verbal and physical assaults administered by midshipmen, officers, instructors, local town people, and Academy visitors. Although the law stated women were not to be placed in combat, many of the women of the class of 1980 became familiar with fighting in order to survive. In addition to what was happening to me, I heard about horrible atrocities being inflicted upon women across the Brigade. Any woman who stood out for her beauty, her brains, or her other attention-garnering characteristics, seemed to be one of the greatest targets.

What I found to be interesting was these women generally did not report the mistreatment. If they got the same reception I did, there was no sense in reporting it to leadership, which appeared duplicitous regarding the mistreatment of women. What amazed me was with all the media attention, no one really reported the details of what we were experiencing to the press. We dealt with it within the Hall.

One of these attacks occurred one crisp autumn afternoon as I was walking on the curved walkway in front of the Chapel heading for Griffin Hall. A rock flew past my head at decapitating speed. I looked in the direction the rock came from. There was a group of white male midshipmen standing on Stribling Walk, looking menacingly in my direction. Other midshipmen were walking by as though nothing had happened. Rock throwing was such a common occurrence, if all else failed, I wondered if they would just resort to stoning me to death.

This had already been a difficult day. I had stayed up most of the night studying for an engineering exam, knowing full well the best grade I could receive was a "B," no matter how well I did on the test. *Officer potential.* I had also been informed by two random "MidshipWorms" that I didn't belong at the Academy—all before noon. I was not in the mood for ignoring anymore mistreatment by the hands of these miscreants. So, I turned and yelled, "Who threw the rock?!" A few people looked in my direction, but quickly continued toward their destinations.

I don't know what I expected. Maybe a brave confession from some guy wanting to make a point of letting me know there was nothing I could do about it. (You wouldn't believe how often this happened. I always made sure the poor, misguided soul paid dearly for his confession. I usually left him lying where he previously stood to throw his rock.)

But this encounter was different. Usually assaults were one-on-one and typically with no witnesses. Maybe the word had gotten out about the failure of previous attacks, so the tactics were changing. No matter the situation, I had to warrior up. Group stoning was not going to become the new alternative. When I yelled again, asking who threw the rock, they laughed. I saw where the large rock landed. It looked like a piece of the walkway that had been kicked loose and pulled from the ground. I walked into the roadway and

Warrior Up

retrieved the stone. I turned and walked back to where I left my books. And then I wound up with a pitch that would have made Jackie Robinson proud, hurling the stone head level, straight into the middle of the group of boys. They dived for cover, cursing as they flew, hurling their usual insults in my directions. As I picked up my books, I dared them to throw it again and promised to beat the ~~shit~~ solid waste out of the one who threw it.

That was my last rock attack.

I didn't go to tell anyone. I didn't depend on anyone else to resolve this issue. I didn't go to the press or demand diversity and inclusion training. Wars, missions, operations could not cease every time someone chose to attack me. I chose to enter a warrior's world. It was up to me to respond as a warrior would. I am by no means justifying their behavior. If I thought it was okay, I would not have tried to take their heads off. What I'm saying is the warrior's world is comprised of victims and victors. All new entrants are tested to ensure they will not fall apart when faced with the real enemy. The unit had to know if all members were ready. If an individual could be intimidated by peers, then it was unlikely they could repel an attack from a true enemy.

At least that's what I was told. I really didn't care what motivated the behavior. They were my enemies. I had to "warrior up" if I intended to graduate. This reflection is about the choices we make, and the responsibilities we assume based on those choices. As midshipmen, we fundamentally choose to be warriors, no matter what additional area of expertise we possess. If we are unwilling or incapable of meeting the warrior's commitments, then we should choose another profession.

Whether I liked my treatment or not, in some strange manner, it kind of made sense. A warrior would be attacked from all fronts. A warrior would need to perform under severe stress. A warrior could not expect to have someone intercede on her behalf when being mistreated by the enemy. A warrior had to be knowledgeable and proficient in the execution of her craft. A warrior understood her responsibility to other warriors and didn't let them down. A warrior had to do whatever was required within established boundaries to accomplish the mission. A warrior had to stand, even if she stood alone. And a warrior should be surrounded by shipmates who made the same commitments to her, the naval service, and the nation.

The fact that my "initiation" was so much more intense than what was required of most of my peers was what I resented. I had proven my willingness and ability to "warrior up." I expected the other midshipmen that chose to attack me to do the same. There is a difference between initiation and persecution. Singling out a member of the unit for ongoing group harassment is the behavior of cowards—not warriors. This was not the behavior the Navy should want from their leaders in the Fleet and Corps. It was not me who still needed to prove I could be a warrior—that responsibility laid squarely on the shoulders of those who continued to persecute others based on their differences. This was an issue of honor, courage, and leadership at its core.

Making choices—and holding ourselves accountable to them—is much easier said than done. As youths, I think we all eventually must decide who we are, what we will do, what we will not do, and what all that means. It's a part of growing up, and these early decisions can often impact the opportunities available to us throughout our lives. Had I been arrested at the party, the Academy may not have even been an option for me.

In the reflection, "What Did You Expect?" I mentioned my gratitude to the senior leader who didn't step in to defend me against all the attacks I was experiencing. Whatever his intention, what he accomplished was to force me to "warrior up." I had to choose between being a victim or a victor. I chose the latter. The United States Naval Academy did not graduate victims. In the spring of 1976, I chose to be a warrior, opening a door at the Academy. This is what I was meant to do — *No Coincidences*.

19 – *What Not to Do*

I think I've learned as much from bad examples as good ones. I was a very observant child. I paid close attention to the words and actions of others as I was growing up. Much to my parent's chagrin, they were often faced with the regurgitation of their own lessons. Since they were not from the "Do as I say, not what I do" school, the regurgitation of their lessons often produced the result I desired.

I not only paid attention to the actions of others, but also the consequences of those actions. I was obsessed with seeing whether what was done or said achieved the intended results. Too often, it did not. Most of the time, the root issue lay in unreconciled objectives. They were communicating one thing when their intent was something else. This was demonstrated to me one morning in elementary school.

I was seen as a leader and the teacher often left the class under my supervision when she had to step out. On this particular day, there was to be an all school assembly. Students in all grades were given a specific time to arrive and be seated. My teacher was called away unexpectedly and asked me to line the class up and take them to the auditorium if she didn't return on time. She provided specific instructions regarding how to line up, which side of the corridor to walk on, the requirement to remain quiet, which door to enter, and where to sit.

I listened closely, determined to do a good job if needed. I wanted her to know her faith in me was well placed. The

What Not to Do

teacher left, and we worked on the assignment she provided. When the time came for the class to proceed to the auditorium, she had not returned. I pulled out my notes, let my classmates know what we needed to do, lined them up, and proceeded to the auditorium as instructed. When we arrived at the assigned door it was chained. Unsure of what to do, I knocked on it. I don't know why I thought this would help, but there was no response. Since this was not the only door to the auditorium, I led my classmates around the corner to another door. We were the first class to arrive. The only person in the auditorium was the school administrator. He was furious.

Seeing I was leading the class and getting everyone seated, he approached me and asked who told me to come in that door. He said we were supposed to enter in the door around the corner. He asked if I knew that, but all he would let me get out was, "Yes, I know we were supposed to use the other door, but…" Before I could say another word, he pulled me by the arm to the front of the auditorium.

I began my elementary education in a school for black children. Corporal punishment was still alive and well. As the school administrator pulled me to front, he released a tirade of accusations against me. He said I thought I was in charge and that I was better than other people. He said I thought the rules didn't apply to me and I could do as I d*mn well pleased. Every time I tried to explain what happened, he told me to shut up. He said he was going to finally give me what I deserved.

What Not to Do

My teacher walked in as he pulled a paddle with holes in it from behind the podium and was pulling up a chair. He intended to put me over his lap and paddle me. She came in yelling, asking what was going on, but he told her to be quiet too. He said he was going to straighten me out. I was confused and crying, but I knew I had done nothing to deserve this.

Just as he pulled me to him in the chair and was picking up the paddle to hit me, I snatched it from his hand. I hit him beside the head with all my might and took off running. He was not far behind me, screaming my name. I hit the exit door at full speed, ran outside and down the hill to the high school for black children. My mother was the librarian there.

By the time I came storming into the library, I could barely speak. Mama was overseeing a study hall and working with some student assistants on an audiovisual need. She looked at me in horror. Between gasping for air and crying, I was unable to answer her questions. She left one of her students in charge and took me out in the hall to a common area with chairs. She listened attentively as I explained to her what happened.

I was so upset. I didn't know why the school administrator had behaved that way. What had I done wrong? Also, I couldn't believe I had hit him. My father was adamant about not allowing a man to hit me. He said if I did require discipline, ask for a woman—emphasizing that had better not ever happen. My mother was the one who spanked me.

What Not to Do

My father never physically disciplined me. He didn't need to. I was Daddy's Girl.

My mother explained to me it wasn't my fault; the man was angry about a recent altercation she had with him in which he was disciplined. He was taking it out on me. She was furious. She went to the office and explained she needed to leave briefly to take care of something at the elementary school. (There was no middle school back then.) My mother didn't say a word as she drove up the street to the school, but she was beet red and her jaw was clinched. By the time I came back, assembly was over, and she sent me to my class. She assured me I would never have a problem with him again. (Actually, I don't believe I ever saw him again.)

This experience taught me not to take out my aggressions on innocent people in order to make a point with others with whom I was angry. Also, never underestimate the innocent person. Although I may cause some initial discomfort, it was not likely to end well for me—I could get a paddle upside my head. It was not a coincidence I was able to use this lesson at the Academy.

I have always found it interesting people assumed I would wrongly do to them what they knew was wrongly done to me—payback. Many white male midshipmen knew as a black female, I was catching hell from people who looked just like them. When I was placed in a position of authority over them, they responded with abject horror.

As Plebe Summer Regimental Adjutant, I was a

What Not to Do

"midshipman officer." The three stripes on my uniform indicated my level of authority. I was in a position to provide guidance to other Firsties as well as plebes. I could see people watching to see if I would behave as my elementary school administrator did—vengefully punishing the innocent based on my unresolved anger. Their concern even translated to my interactions with the plebes.

Although I was not responsible for the day to day development of plebes, my classmates from my company would occasionally send down a poorly performing plebe for "course correction." Apparently, I was being billed as the destination of last recourse, and it was a trip from which a plebe would not return unscathed. I probably only saw two or three plebes—I guess the threat was enough. The one raising the most eyebrows and ire was a plebe who had disrespected a first-class female.

I braced him up against the wall and began to verbally disassemble every arrogant portion of his anatomy. His smug smirk was soon replaced by his tears and his resounding declaration that I would never need to have this conversation with him again. I promised him the next time would not be so pleasant.

What was interesting was the entire hall had filled with other first-class midshipmen observing the interaction and the loud lecture I gave him regarding his oath of office, the military chain of command, and the consequences for disobedience of lawful orders. Sprinkled within these

What Not to Do

military instructions were comments equating his behavior and intellect to a jackass. (We did that back then—just for effect.) I was in his face screaming at him. At the end of our "discussion," I told him I had better never see him again under these circumstances.

He requested permission to return to his company area. I told him to report to the first-class female, explain to her why what he had done was inappropriate, and assure her it would never happen again. I was told he did as he was instructed, and the problem did not reoccur. As he turned to "chop" (run) away, I calmly turned to enter my room. I wasn't angry. I was just doing my job.

So, what about the other Firsties who witnessed this? Some appeared to be in shock. Others told me they wanted to cry, too. It was because they had never seen a black female—or any female, as they put it—verbally castrate a large white male. (Oh yeah, I forgot to mention he was a *big* boy.) They struggled with what they witnessed, but no one accused me of taking revenge for past atrocities. That was not me, anyway. That behavior fell into the "What Not to Do" category. The "What Not to Do" behaviors I experienced from my school administrator and others throughout my youth were my most prolific sources of instruction — *No Coincidences*.

20 – Motivation

I learned very early in life not to be reactionary, but to figure out what was driving the behaviors I was witnessing. That sounds like a strange behavior for a kid but, remember, I had been going into places where I was considered an oddity since I was eight years old. I had to understand why the other kids responded to me as they did.

So, what were the other kids' responses to me as an "alien" among them? They excluded me. They talked *about* me instead of *to* me. They paid close attention to their property when I approached them. And they *assumed* I was ignorant and only in their presence because I was filling the elusive quota. I was one of "those" people. Imagine how that felt.

Their behavior left me with multiple options. I could treat them the way they treated me—but that is how ignorance begets ignorance. I could get angry and decide if they thought I was so bad, I would just show them what "bad" really looked like! Again, the ignorance monster would have reigned supreme. I could be quiet and retreat, going in search of anyone who looked like me. Or, I could try to change the mindsets that spawned these behaviors.

In a previous reflection, I mentioned that my father taught me about the deliberate misinformation perpetrated regarding the intellect, character, and behavior of black people. So, I had a sense of what I was dealing with. But the main thing I remembered about what he said was how black people and white people were mutually being deprived of the opportunity to get to know each other—the opportunity to become friends. Being the little crusader I was, I decided to take it upon myself to overcome generations of family training, media misinformation, biased interpretation of scripture being delivered in churches, and a general belief that black people hated white people because of slavery. (Do you know any slaves? Me either. I always found that belief interesting. If black people are racist, they don't have to reach back hundreds of years to try to justify it. Anyway, I digress.)

Looking back, I must have been a rather "cheeky" kid to believe I could overcome these very strong motivators. I think my Invisible Friends always gave me the confidence to do the right thing without really focusing on how difficult it would be. I would like to say I studied the problem and defined a detailed plan to change the behaviors of the other kids by addressing their motivations. But that was not the case. I just decided to be me.

I acted as though I was not being ignored. I joined in conversations. I participated in class and after-school events. I had very good grades and offered to help the other kids. I shared my things. I had great snacks at school. I listened to problems and helped if I could. I kept secrets. I just behaved like any other kid.

The initial reaction was what one would expect if someone released a stink bomb in a crowd. They let me know I was not welcome—more through facial expressions and body language than direct comments. I persisted, and their

Motivation

resolve began to erode. They began to actually talk to me. (You're not going to believe what they said.) Comments like, "I don't really like black people, but you're not really a black person. You don't act like them. I like you."

Okay, again I had several options I could have chosen in response to this comment. As you might imagine, they were not all positive. But I was actually excited to hear this comment. It was the first direct communication of the feelings they harbored and a crack in the wall of their beliefs—the insidious beliefs that motivated their negative behavior toward blacks. So, my choice in responding to one young girl was to engage her in a discussion. I said, "Thank you? I like you, too. Do you know a lot of black people?" With an almost look of disgust on her face, she said, "No. You're the only one." So, I asked, "Then how do you know you don't like black people? You only know one, and you like me." I will never cease to be surprised by her response, even though I have heard it numerous times throughout my life. "But you're not really black," she said. "You're not like those other people." Again, I asked, very calmly and patiently, "If you don't know any of those other people, how do you know what they're like?"

I was not trying to trip her up or make her feel uncomfortable. I wanted the discussion to continue. We could not produce sustainable change (my adult words) unless we allowed each other to honestly share our fears, feelings, trainings, or beliefs that motivate our behaviors—no matter how offensive they may be. She explained she knew about other black people based on what her parents said and what she saw on the television. Black people are criminals. My father's words began to echo in my head. I explained to her, if I'm a good black person and I'm the only one she knows, then there probably are other good black people like me. I suggested she should consider giving each one a chance to show her who they were before she decided she didn't like them. I could tell she was struggling with what I said, so I just changed the subject in order to give her time to think about it.

Later that week, she approached me and said, "I'll give it a try." I looked at her quizzically, and asked, "You'll try what?" She said, "I will give black people a chance, but if one of them bothers me, I'm coming to you for protection. But I'm not going to tell my parents. They're not ready to give black people a chance yet." This was a huge step for a little girl. I assured her I would not let anyone hurt her. It's funny because she really did that after forced integration occurred. She let people know I was her black friend—and they had better not bother her. She also eventually introduced me to her parents. She was cute. Change is a process.

Her acceptance opened the door and I had similar conversations with other children. It was not always easy to listen to their insulting comments and tolerate their condescending behavior. But I focused on their motivation. They didn't mean to be insulting or condescending. They were just being honest based on what they had been taught.

I learned a lot from my foray into carrying the burden of my

Motivation

entire race to change the attitudes of a bunch of elementary kids. This didn't require a performance because I was a true believer black people were wonderful. Initially, I thought my new friends only needed exposure. I soon learned this was not enough. We had to be able to directly communicate about what motivated our behaviors. Not easy, especially for a bunch of kids on the playground. But it was a piece of cake compared to the Academy. My youth was full of those types of interchanges and the experiences were invaluable at the Academy.

The comments about women not belonging at the Academy were too numerous to mention. But only in quantity—the actual comments were very similar. "You can't lead men!" "You're just here filling a quota, taking a spot from a man!" "You can't serve in combat, so why are you here?" "You're dumb." "You're stupid." "You're ugly!" *Blah, blah, blah, yada, yada, yada*. It was all the same stuff. I heard it from midshipmen, instructors, professors, and even civilians! Apparently, everyone had opinions and felt the need to express them—often.

So just like on the playground in Aiken, South Carolina, I had options. I thought I could show them better than I could tell them, but just like when I was a child, that was only step one. And anyway, it wasn't like the playing field would be even. Can I really show them my abilities when I wasn't given the grades I earned? But again, that would not have been enough anyway. We needed to talk. I needed to understand their motivation.

Motivation

The Academy was a different place in 1976. Your mental, moral, and physical abilities within the context of sound leadership were constantly under assessment. If you were found wanting, it was strongly suggested you pursue another career. The Brigade of Midshipman had a lot to do with persuading you to leave. The Academy was tasked with ensuring only high-performing officers reached the Fleet. Retention was not a part of the Academy's active vocabulary.

With this context in mind, coupled with the kind words of acceptance I received on a regular basis (just kidding!), some midshipmen saw it as their professional responsibility to ensure I didn't reach the Fleet. This unwavering focus on the mission of the Academy—combined with the same misinformation my playground friends operated under—motivated the midshipmen to try to run me out. They believed they were unquestionably right. Even though Congress and the President of the United States—dual-hatted as the Commander in Chief—mandated I should be there, they felt they knew better than these "outsiders." Their belief they were right was so strong they felt obligated to resist any affront to their "rightness." I called it righteous indignation.

How do you combat this type of motivation, almost fanatical in its nature, especially when it is covertly supported by some of the leaders at the highest levels of government, and the military to whom these young men were very loyal? It was too much for a 19-year-old black girl from Aiken, South Carolina to process. It was like standing against principalities. There is no way I could have succeeded against such powerful, complex, and widespread motivation, all focused on getting me out.

It's great to have Invisible Friends who never leave me alone, guide my every step, and shelter me from realities that are more than I can handle. They also sent the quiet angels that allowed me to show I was worthy. The black battalion officer who guided my last years, the kind senior officer who understood why I went to the party (I'll explain this later), and the political science professor who always gave me my earned grade will always be angels to me. I will never forget them. Those who put me in positions of responsibility in order to demonstrate I could lead. Although showing them was not sufficient in and of itself, I had to at least be able to demonstrate my mental, moral, and physical capability before I could get them to talk to me. Again, discussions were needed to challenge their motivating beliefs—beliefs driving them to perceive I represented, minimally, a threat to good order and discipline, and ultimately a threat to national defense.

So how did I take it beyond just showing them? The same way I did on the playground. I focused on my most ardent adversaries and allowed them to talk. First, I had to fight them toe-to-toe. We were all operating outside the rules. Like I said, it was war, and the rules of engagement didn't apply. I met them where they were and interestingly enough, they respected that. We began to talk.

Now, I'm not saying these initial discussions were fruitful.

Motivation

Most of them contained quite a few four-letter words, violent threats, unkind remarks regarding unnatural parental interactions, and—more often than I care to remember—strong references to the female of the canine species. One day after a particularly heated conversation with my most tenacious adversary, he just stared at me for a while and asked, "Why won't you just leave?" Thinking we were still in the middle of our verbal war, I said, "I ask myself the same thing about *you* every day, you blankety, blank, blank blank!" He said, "No, really, I'm serious." I was about to say, "I'm serious, too!" when I finally looked in his face and saw something different. Something I'd never seen there before. He just looked tired. I was cautiously excited. Had we finally moved beyond "sparring" to actually "communicating?"

We had. So, I began to answer his question. I told him members of my family had served this nation in uniform since World War II. That an older male cousin was now serving in the Marines and that was what I wanted to do. That attending the Academy allowed me to achieve many objectives simultaneously. I could serve my nation, obtain an excellent education, increase my leadership skills, grow up fast, understand how to perform under stress, and I needed to open this door. If I was the only one to be admitted, I needed to come, survive, perform, and graduate. People needed to know black women were capable, willing, and ready to serve and based on all my other life experiences, I believed I was prepared to lead this change.

He asked me many more questions over multiple meetings.

Motivation

He listened to me—and I listened to him explain why he felt I shouldn't be there. He shared some of the same misconceptions as my playground friends, but he also made legitimate points about the current condition of the Navy and Marine Corps—that the naval service was no place for "people like me." I told him organizations seldom willingly accept significant change that was thrust upon them. But, resist as they might, change still occurs. Change is the only constant. And whether people liked it or not, it was coming. I asked, "Can you just give this change a chance?"

He never answered that question. But he never treated me badly again. When his behavior changed, the behavior of others changed. We had dealt with our differences by dealing with the issues that drove those differences—our motivations. And, just like the little girl on the playground, he was willing to give it a chance — *No Coincidences*.

21 – *Trust, Then Verify*

When most of us take over a new position or responsibility, one of our first actions is to discuss the job with someone who has done it before. It's great to be provided with insights by someone with experience to walk us through the expectations of the new task. If we're lucky, in addition to the job description, there are also written policies and procedures that spelled out how the duties are to be performed.

That was my hope when I started my first paying job in a popular retail outlet in Aiken. The owner was a tall, dark-haired, handsome white man who was very exacting. He required things be done right—the first time. We were well paid, and he demanded outstanding performance. I learned a lot from him—not only about retail operations, but also about customer service. He was always pleasant as he listened attentively to the needs of his customers, patiently providing just the right product for the occasion as well as the personal budget. He showed me in order to achieve your goals, you must take care of the people. That's probably why my daddy chose him to be my first employer.

My daddy got the job for me. As soon as I turned sixteen, he took me to the store, introduced me to the owner, and told me to do a good job. I was to report there after school activities and before karate lessons on the nights when they occurred. I also worked on Saturdays unless there was a karate tournament. No work on Sundays. My daddy would not stand for that. My first assignment was behind the perfume and makeup counter with Brenda.

Brenda was a grown woman. She had worked at the store for years and was the resident perfume and makeup expert. She was assigned to train me on management of this counter as well as general store operations. It was obvious I was on a probationary period by her constant use of veiled threats regarding my future employment if I messed up. I was the first person who looked like me ever to work on the main floor of the store. I could tell Brenda had reservations about whether or not I was up to the task.

I never knew there was so much involved in managing a store. As a young customer, I never thought about where the products came from, how they magically appeared on the shelves, what was involved in pricing, and who designed those nice displays that caught my eye as soon as I walked in the store. As a new employee, I thought about it now and it was *not* magical. It was a lot of hard work.

Brenda was a reluctant trainer. She was professional, but not very friendly. I guess training teenagers was not exactly her idea of fun, but I was totally dependent upon her to be successful in my new job. I couldn't disappoint my new employer, and even more importantly, my daddy.

Brenda provided instructions rapidly and had little patience for questions. She told me how to go to the storeroom and restock shelves, paying attention to expiration dates. She shared her ideas about how to design attractive displays and which products should be highlighted, and when. She instructed me on reorders and inventory management. Using the cash register was easy. I was good at math, calculating change and "what if" amounts in my head came easily. "Cleanliness was next to Godliness" behind Brenda's counter. Pricing remained my final hurdle.

I think Brenda provided pricing training last because she personally found it most challenging. Pricing in a retail outlet is the core of successful operations. This store often put marketing flyers in the paper, highlighting certain products and announcing sales. The sale prices had to reflect decreases attractive enough to bring shoppers to the store, while not too greatly impacting the profitability. We needed to have initial pricing that exceeded total product cost enough to later permit attractive sales while still generating the desired profit.

Brenda's instructions were quick and cryptic. I was still very unsure of what was required. Although I wrote down what she said, her verbal instructions didn't clearly explain how to determine the appropriate price to charge and when items should be discounted. I asked her if there were written instructions. She said she thought there was "something" written down "somewhere," although she didn't know where to find it and more importantly, why was I unable to understand her instructions and just perform the task?

Brenda's response left me feeling as though I had to prove I wasn't stupid and should just proceed with the instructions I was given. The store owner thought highly of Brenda, and I was concerned that if I went to him, she would convince him I was stupid. I just couldn't lose my first job and disappoint my daddy. So, when the new order of expensive perfume came in and Brenda asked me to price it, I applied my limited knowledge to the assignment. This first stage was simple because it involved a straight percentage markup. The challenge arose with the periodic markdowns and sales.

The new perfume proved to be a slow mover. People were unwilling to pay the initial price, which did include a healthy 30% markup. The decision was made to lower the price to be more comparable with the prices in the larger department stores. This still represented a healthy profit. The price decrease resulted in increased sales, but inventory levels remained higher than desired. With the approach of the holiday season, this was the perfect opportunity to significantly increase perfume sales and use the product to lure additional customers into the store.

I was told by Brenda to lower the price by 20% more. I questioned the significant price decrease and said it offered very little profit. I was basically told to do as instructed and not challenge management decisions. So, I lowered the price by 20% more. This was advertised as part of our holiday sales, and we had a stampede of customers at the perfume counter.

The store owner came by at the end of the first day of the sale period and commented on how well the sale was going based on how many people were at the counter during the day. I said the perfume we had on sale was very popular,

Trust, Then Verify

and we were basically giving it away. "I sure hope we're getting additional sales on other items from the people who came to buy the perfume," I said. An immediate look of concern came over his face, and he said, "What do mean, 'basically free?'" I told him we had already lowered the price to what other stores were charging, and then lowered it by another 20% more, which basically erased the initial 30% markup and took the price below the initial cost of buying the perfume.

He hit the roof! Brenda came running over to where we were standing. The store owner asked us what we had done. Brenda quickly explained I was the one who had priced the product. He looked at her like she was stupid, and then asked me to explain what I had done. When I finished he just stared at Brenda, asking what I had done incorrectly. She just stared back at him, and I sheepishly asked, "Was I supposed to decrease the price based on the original price we first started with?" He said, "Exactly!" He asked me why I didn't follow instructions. I showed him my written notes based on Brenda's instructions. He looked at me quizzically and pulled back the sliding doors to a cabinet behind the counter. I never went under this cabinet because it was where Brenda kept "her things." (It was a mess under there.) He pulled out all the miscellaneous items, and in the back on the bottom was a binder of store operating instructions.

He stated flatly there was no need to ask if I had ever seen this binder. Brenda explained she didn't know it was there, and she hadn't seen it for years. He was very upset he was

Trust, Then Verify

selling product at a loss. Even though he put most of the blame on Brenda, he did ask me, "If you knew it was being sold below cost, why didn't you say anything?" Brenda didn't speak up and admit I did say something, and unwilling to through her under the bus, I just apologized and said it wouldn't happen again. He calmed down. I think he could tell by our body language what had occurred.

He handed the binder to me, and I promised to study the contents overnight and use it as a constant reference guide going forward. To my surprise, he quickly took the binder back, stating, "I think I'd better update this and make sure all employees are using it." And that was exactly what he did.

I no longer had to depend on Brenda for instructions and I soon had a counter of my own. From this experience I learned to trust those assigned to provide skills and guidance, but to always ask for the materials they used as the basis of their instructions—trust, then verify.

At the Academy, one of my first acts was to study the thick blue binder of instructions and regulations—the MHP (Midshipman Held Publication). Brenda taught me an invaluable lesson.

The MHP covered topics like the daily schedule, uniform requirements, liberty guidelines, behavioral expectations, privileges based on class, maintenance of rooms, use of facilities, and general administration like leave procedures. This binder was prominently displayed in each dormitory

Trust, Then Verify

room. By the time I got to my room, the fact I was *very* unwelcome had been clearly and consistently communicated to me. Also, there would be no hesitation in doing whatever it took to persuade me my decision to attend the Academy was not in anyone's best interest. Especially mine. I would need to become very familiar with the MHP.

I thought if I at least knew the rules, I could perform two very important tasks: 1) comply with all requirements and avoid the demerits that would cause me to spend all my free time marching, and 2) know when I was being dealt with in a manner outside of these rules. If I knew when my antagonist was committing an infraction, and I knew what my options were under the rules, I could make intelligent decisions regarding how to respond. And oh, by the way, just telling them they were not in compliance wasn't one of those options. Remember, no one cared. And from a previous reflection, "What did I expect when I came here?"

An important part of Academy life—as well as an extremely critical regulation—was the Honor Concept. The Honor Concept states, "A midshipman will not lie, cheat, or steal." This concept differs from the West Point Honor Code, where the last line stated, "…nor tolerate any cadet who does." This was not part of the Naval Academy concept in order to give the infringing midshipman a chance to repent and remain honorable. The midshipman witnessing the Honor Concept violation had the options of providing counsel, providing counsel *and* reporting the incident, or just reporting the midshipman violating the Honor Concept. Avoiding an honor violation was like escaping the plague.

No one wanted to be labeled as dishonorable. This was a sure condition that could result in prompt dismissal from the Brigade of Midshipmen.

One might think it is simple to not lie, cheat, or steal, but as usual, the devil is in the details. Completion of fully annotated academic work was required to avoid an honor violation. Footnotes, bibliographies, references—all had to be perfectly documented. Also, the restatement of information in general terms based on concepts derived from the research had to be written in your own words with your adaptation of the meaning of the texts. This was a case in which the rule book provided a general behavioral expectation as well as the intent, but not the literary specifics. This information was contained in supplemental guidance that might vary based on the professor.

In high school, I wrote many papers and was familiar with documenting the sources of my information, but the Academy required an exactness I had not experienced. Additionally, there was no single established standard that was consistently applied by all professors. I knew this was a potential avenue that could be leveraged to remove me from the student body unless I was very careful.

Having said this, all my papers were written the night before they were due. I would ponder them for days. Collect reference materials. Envision an outline with the critical content and the resulting knowledge derived from this endeavor. But the paper was written at the last possible minute to allow an accomplished typist to complete the task and receive the appropriate remuneration. This left little time for speculating on the proper source annotation.

For my first paper at the Academy, the professor provided reference material regarding source annotation as well as directed us to some books that further elaborated on the topic. My challenge was using information from magazines and newspapers. The guidance on documenting this material was particularly fluid and confusing. My topic was a current topic, versus an old, established concept with many well-reviewed texts. Newspapers and magazines were important to establishing the contemporary thought regarding the topic. As I started to work on the paper, I wished my professor had warned me about the pitfalls of this kind of topic.

Based on guidance I received from a midshipman who had completed this course, I decided to restate and summarize the current thoughts and developments without annotation. He said he didn't know of anyone who used these sources, but since they were not established academic or material facts, I should just summarize this information without annotation. Made sense to me.

As I was writing my paper in preparation for the typist, Brenda came to mind. I went back to look at the professor's guidance again and was still unsure of how to proceed. Looking up information back then was an arduous task involving finding the right book based on content type, then looking through the book to unearth the single bit of information needed before moving forward. *I don't have time to research source annotations!* But, if there was a question, I chose to err on the side of too much documentation.

I gave the paper to the typist and headed for the library. I thought if anyone would know the answer to my question, it would be a librarian. I ran all the way. I had to get to the library, identify the most commonly accepted source annotations for newspapers and magazines, run back to the Hall, and update the paper allowing the typist to finish, all in less than ninety minutes. In ninety minutes, plebes had to be in bed. And the paper was due the next morning.

As I breathlessly and frantically approached the librarian's desk, I asked for her assistance. She shushed me and asked that I calm down and tell her what I needed. I explained my concern, asking if magazines and newspaper articles should be individually annotated in my paper. She said they should be referenced, and it was always better to be safe than sorry when it came to avoiding honor violations. I quickly responded, questioning where I could find instructions on how to document theses sources in my paper.

She slowly rose and went to the card catalogue to show me how to find books on this topic. I explained I didn't have time for the typical librarian approach to assisting midshipmen in their quest for knowledge. I just wanted her to tell me, based on her vast experience, which book(s) would provide the information I needed in a commonly accepted Academy format. I could tell there was an internal struggle going on inside her regarding whether she should submit to this unusual request. It was at this point I pulled out the big guns, looked her squarely in her face, and loudly said, "Please?" Time was not on my side, and I was not beyond begging.

A look of amusement spread across her face as she shushed me again and led me directly to the book I needed. I squeezed her hand and expressed my undying gratitude as I checked out the book. I returned to the typist, made the additions, and got to bed with mere minutes to spare.

In class the next day, the professor asked me how I dealt with the more current events contents in my paper. He asked about my sources and how I portrayed the information. Then he asked me to show him my citations. I sensed he was somewhat surprised by what he saw. He said he wondered how I was going to handle this information in my paper and if I would properly annotate it. I asked if what I did was okay. He seemed to reluctantly respond that it would do.

I was happy to accept the "reluctant" validation. But I was most happy I remembered the lesson I learned from Brenda. If I had listened to the midshipman, I would have been reported for being in violation of the Honor Concept based on plagiarism. Instead, I got a "B" on my paper and survived another day. Thank you, Brenda — *No Coincidences*.

22 – Heroes

Integration in Aiken, South Carolina schools was managed with little disruption. My mother was very active in ensuring it worked for everyone. Having attended traditionally white schools for years, integration was largely a "non-event" for me—except now there were many more black students, and this was a change. Most of the other black children had gone to school together and knew each other, so I was an outsider to that group.

And as might be expected, there were comments about me "acting white," "sounding white," and "thinking I was white." What offended me about these comments was the underlying message that if a person was well behaved and articulate, then they were "white." I adamantly informed them this was typical of a "slave mentality," and they should be saying things to lift their people up—not tear them down. And most importantly, I stated, "If you can't find anything good to say, then keep your mouth shut!" After that encounter, no one said things like that anymore. At least not to my face.

I was starting high school, integration was underway, and with my mother being very active in the process, people either loved her or hated her. Many teachers were having a more difficult time transitioning than the students. I was dealing with multiple issues associated with all of these changes. The most challenging issues were with some of the teachers.

Those in authority over a group of people have the ability to impact the self-esteem and performance of members of the group. We hoped these leaders would fulfill these implied duties to assist in the development of strong, capable individuals. Unfortunately, this is not always the case. I refer to these duties as "implied" because teachers weren't required to take responsibility for the full development of the child. They were only required to teach their particular subject—and move on.

This sense of responsibility for the "whole person" in teaching was a casualty of integration. Teachers became very sensitive to counseling and correcting children due to the fear of being labeled racist or getting "out of their place." Many just stuck to straight teaching except with those students with whom they were comfortable. This comfort level tended to form along racial lines. Most of the teachers in my high school were white, so the extra attention and guidance black students received in school prior to integration was no longer available. Black students were accustomed to formal titles, rules, and discipline reinforced by strong corporal punishment. (In short, if you messed up in black schools, they would beat your behind.) The loss of this parental reinforcement based on this new hands-off philosophy was a significant loss to the black culture.

Experienced teachers are able to quickly define individual learning styles among students—if they choose to. By understanding the learning style, the teacher could make it easier—or more difficult—for the student. Frequently, teachers used examples not all students could relate to,

Heroes

didn't recognize the raised hand of certain students, asked questions in a manner that was more difficult for some children to answer, and graded tests on a sliding scale—being harsher with some students than others.

There are many more examples of how a person in authority can insidiously destroy the confidence and capability of those under their charge. Their behaviors not only impact the individual, but lead others to believe the person is inferior based on leadership responses, further supporting unfavorable stereotypes. I witnessed this—and experienced it—as I transitioned through high school. The effect on me was significantly mitigated by the proximity of my mother and the teachings of my father. In a previous reflection, I mentioned he "schooled" me at an early age about mind control. For the most part, I knew it when I saw it, and took countermeasures to hamper the teacher's detrimental plans for me.

Fortunately, most teachers didn't subscribe to this intentional destructive behavior. They just taught the subject and interacted with students with whom they felt comfortable. This was understandable. These were challenging times. But a few teachers stepped up and met the challenge. They continued to be concerned about the whole person and didn't let societal pressures destroy their passion to shape young minds. They were the heroes.

So, what made them my heroes? They talked to me. They listened to my ideas and allowed me to challenge conventional wisdom in class. They not only included but encouraged me. I could tell they were excited by my responses, and they engaged me in lively debates. I loved it! In addition to inculcating these critical skills in me, they demonstrated the positive use of positional authority. I was also blessed with heroes that demonstrated these same qualities and were there for me just when I needed them at the Academy.

Most of my instructors and professors at the Academy ignored me. I think they ignored most of the female midshipmen. A few were openly hostile, but I've already told you about them. One was a gem because he did the same things that made me value those teachers in high school. I think what made him most impactful was he provided a caring intellectual and developmental experience in an environment that was almost totally void of any human caring. At least in high school, I had my family and friends to interact with every day. Those negative experiences in high school represented only a small portion of my life. At the Academy, I faced exactly the opposite situation. Negativity was the preponderance of my day. The rare pleasant experience with this professor was something I looked forward to with great anticipation.

It's not that every moment at the Academy was miserable. Many of the moments were—well—nothing. It reminded me of an Academy adaptation of the first *Alien* movie tagline, "In Bancroft Hall, No One Can Hear You Scream." Or, maybe Thoreau said it best: "The mass of men lead lives of quiet desperation." That's a better description of what it was like. I probably was not the only one who felt that way.

This all went away when I entered this particular professor's classroom.

I almost ran to his class on the days when it graced my schedule. I was "uber" prepared for intense discussion and debate. I knew I would leave the class better than I entered it. I would be allowed to talk, laugh, and debate with my classmates all in the pursuit of higher learning and character development. I wasn't just included, I was valued. I was happy there. No more quiet desperation. He was a true role model of how to bring out the best in people and help them to grow.

This professor was not my only hero. A senior military officer who had a choice of how to deal with a debatable decision I made, touched my life in ways he will never know.

It all started with a party. The Seventh Battalion of black midshipmen threw the best parties, and all were welcome, including the plebes. Even me. The party was going to be on the outskirts of town, so we would need a ride. This sounds like no big deal, except plebes were not allowed to ride in cars. I was so excited. Some of the Firsties made me feel like I was a real midshipman—like I was one of them. Even though I knew many of the black males didn't feel that way. Not really, they just felt sorry for me. That was fine with me. Whatever motivated them to include me didn't matter. I was over the top happy to be able to go out in town and just have fun with other people.

Heroes

The event was well organized. We had to pay cover charges in advance and certain Firsties volunteered to drive the underclassmen to the event. There was food, and dancing, and alcohol. My classmates danced with me all night. (Probably because they didn't have dates. Plebes were also not allowed to date.) I didn't over analyze it. I just had a ball. This was an opportunity to get to know my classmates and make friends.

Just like Cinderella's Ball, it was soon time for the plebes to leave. We all piled back into the designated cars and returned to the Hall. I was in heaven and nothing anyone said or did was going to change that. Well, almost anyone.

The next day, I was summoned to my Company Officer's office and asked whether I participated in this unsanctioned party. I admitted I did, and I was told to report to a senior leader's office to receive my sentencing. I knew the rules and if he was fair, my punishment should have been minimal. But I didn't know what to expect and based on previous interactions with people at his level, I didn't think this would go well. I remembered: *What did I expect when I came here?*

When the day of reckoning arrived, and I reported to the assigned office, I found myself in good company. I recognized many of the party-goers lined up against the wall awaiting their time with the senior leader. I thought it interesting that he chose to handle it this way instead of leaving the punishments to each individual company officer. I didn't know whether this was good or bad. It depended on what was occurring behind those closed doors.

I watched each black midshipman enter and leave without comment. We already knew a plebe had gotten drunk, returned to the Hall, and spilled the beans. He mentioned everyone he could remember and, of course, I was on the list. I felt kind of sorry for him because he had done the unpardonable. He was getting upperclassmen "fried." I was musing about his probable short life expectancy as a member of the Brigade when I realized I was next in line.

As I stepped in front of the open door about to request permission to enter, the leader's assistant told me to come in. I marched in sharply, stood at attention, stared straight ahead, and said, "Midshipman Mines, reporting as ordered, sir!" My eyes were staring straight ahead—as was required for all plebes—but I could still see him. He looked tired as he sat there and just stared at me. Finally, he asked if I attended a party last Saturday night in town. My response was, "Sir, yes, sir!" He said this was in violation of the rules and then asked me why I attended. *What? Did he really just ask me why? Was this a trick?* I just responded in the prescribed manner saying, "No excuse, sir!" In a very exasperated tone, he said, "No, really. I want you to tell me why." I was totally confused and just stared straight ahead. The he demanded, "Look at me! Why did you attend that party?"

I thought to myself, *I have to obey*, so I looked at him and said, "Sir, it wasn't against the rules to attend a party during

Heroes

an approved liberty period. I didn't drink and although I danced with my classmates, I didn't fraternize with or date anyone. And although I rode in a car—which *was* a violation—I didn't go beyond the prohibited seven-mile limit." When he cut me off, I knew I was dead meat. He said, "It's good you know the regulations, and decided to very selectively determine which to violate, but you're still not answering my question. *Why* did you choose to violate any of the rules and attend this party?"

He was not going to allow me to get away with a superficial response and let me take what should have been just a few demerits. I gave up and decided I had to tell him. I felt the admission would leave me vulnerable to harsh responses that would be very hurtful. But, oh well, I had no choice. I looked him directly in his eyes, and said, "There would be black girls there."

He looked at me like I had slapped him, and said, "What?!" I knew I didn't have much time to explain, so I repeated, "There would be black girls there. They would talk to me. And maybe help me find some place to go and get my hair done. I just wanted to see them…" By the time I finished talking, I realized we were both very emotional about what I said. He actually looked like he understood. He looked at me for a few seconds, and said, "Leave my office, and I'd better not *ever* see you here again!" I was dumb struck. I hesitated, waiting for my demerits, and he repeated the order to leave. I stepped outside the door, squared the corner, and I never returned.

Heroes

He left me fundamentally changed that day. I had to accept that the striking men in the fitted uniforms with all the gold trimmings were not all monsters. He didn't hurt me. This single act of understanding restored my faith in the Academy. I thought maybe, just maybe, they're not all bad. I was so touched by his act of kindness, I went to one of my secret places and just cried. I never wanted to disappoint him again. He would be my hero until the day he died. I cried on that day, too.

These heroes occupy a special place in my heart. Positional authority is a powerful responsibility. Lives can be built—or destroyed—based on the exercise of this authority. My heroes from high school and the Academy have positively impacted the lives of people they've never met, through the lessons they taught me — *No Coincidences*.

23 – Fair

At an early age, I grew to understand "fair" was a relative concept. I learned it is self-defeating to focus on whether or not you are being treated fairly. The concept of fairness is like "a riddle wrapped in a mystery, inside an enigma," according to Winston Churchill circa 1939. Many of us define fairness as being treated the same as others without partiality or being treated justly according to the established rules and norms. Fairness always seems to be based on a comparison to something or someone else.

I think most children's first introduction to the fairness concept occurs when comparing their treatment at the hands of a parent to the treatment of siblings. We pay very close attention to ensure one child doesn't get something the other doesn't receive as well. This worked when my sister and I were very small. There is only a 19-month age difference between my sister and me, so as little girls we liked similar things. We were dressed identically, and we always received the same gifts. But as typical of children, I identified a single bone of contention in my comparison with my sister. She received more of my mother's attention and was not responsible for anything. As the oldest, everything fell on me.

We grew to be very different people. For reasons mentioned in an earlier reflection, my sister initially spent more time inside and I was always outdoors. She liked dolls—and I liked beheading them. I enjoyed children's chemistry and biology sets and toolkits. Although we were still being

Fair

dressed alike, as we aged, our toys and gifts became very different. In true child-like form, we would still compare our gifts. I remember complaining to our parents, "You gave my sister a tall walking doll and all I got was a small chemistry set! That's not fair!"

"Do you want the same gifts as your sister?" my mother asked.

"No," I said, incredulously, "we like different things."

"Fairness is not about being treated the same," she explained, "but being treated justly."

The look on my face let her I know I was confused. "It would be unfair to buy gifts for one child and not the other," she further explained. "That would be unjust. But to buy you both the *same* things in an effort to be impartial would also be unfair to one—or both—of you. Someone would be unhappy."

My mother continued to explain that within our family there existed a set of rules and behavioral expectations applying to everyone. There were also special ones applying to all the children equally. From that perspective, we are treated the same. But how she and my daddy addressed the individual needs of each child could be very different. Treating us the same would be ineffective and lazy parenting. We were a family whose members all had to follow a common set of rules, but as individuals we all needed to be treated in a manner reflecting our individuality. For example, at Christmas we all got gifts, but what we got was based on our desires and our compliance with the family rules. She said this is truly fair.

As a child this concept was difficult for me to understand. Why were my cousins praised for Bs and Cs when I would have been punished? My mother said the rule was to work hard and do the best we could at whatever we did. This meant as individuals, there would be things we each did better than one another. She said once our potential was established, we were expected to live up to it and always do our individual best. This still didn't sit quite right with me—I liked things black and white, one size fit all. This customized treatment within the rules was a little too deep for my young mind. As I grew older, I saw other examples and the concept grew clearer.

Sometimes, it was difficult to distinguish between unfair, ineffective, or just plain lazy—like my mom had explained one-size-fits-all parenting. Since I was educated in gifted classes one might think my teachers were creative in understanding different learning styles and adjusting instruction to be as inclusive as possible. Well, no. Jeremy, a new boy in our advanced science class was having difficulty remembering the key concepts. The teacher basically just read the text to us, and I highlighted whatever was emphasized and memorized it for the test.

Jeremy would ask the teacher to explain concepts. Her response was to repeat what she said previously—but louder and slower. In desperation, Jeremy asked if I would

Fair

explain it. I quickly realized he needed pictures and metaphorical stories. He had to visualize the material. Once I did this for him, he picked up the concepts with ease.

I was so excited to explain this to the teacher until I received an unexpected response. The teacher said the material had to be taught the same way to all the students. That way it was consistent and fair for everyone. In my naivety, I asked if pictures and elaborative comments could be included for all of us. That would still be consistent and would probably include more learning styles.

I could tell the teacher was becoming impatient and a bit angry. The response was it would be unfair to change the teaching style in the middle of the course to accommodate one student. I wanted to say Jeremy was in good company because most of the class had Cs, but I knew I was beating a dead horse. This teacher used fairness and consistency to hide the unwillingness—or inability—to meet the needs of individual students.

My mother and this teacher taught me critical lessons about fairness. While the rules apply to everyone, achieving the objectives of those rules often requires an individualized approach. Yes, the rules required all students be taught the same material, but what was the objective? Was it the consistent delivery of the information, or was it to enable the students to learn and apply the information? I think it was the latter. If so, was it fair to teach Jeremy—and about half the class—in a manner unconducive to their learning?

Fair

This concept that consistency is only a part of fairness and leaders will not always work in an identical manner with different people to achieve a common goal was an impactful lesson. And more importantly, this was not unfair. I was fortunate to have had these childhood experiences. This learning was critical as I developed my leadership skills at the Academy.

And then there was Midshipman Gibbs. He was a bright young man from the northeastern part of the country. Top of his class in high school, excellent athlete, Eagle Scout—and totally neurotic. As I returned with the rest of the Brigade to start my Firstie year, I was inundated with "Gibbs stories." All plebes were provided a book of rates, called *Reef Points*, containing material they needed to memorize and recite upon demand. Apparently, Gibbs was consistently failing at this task.

As squad leaders, we met and discussed the plebes. Based on Gibbs' performance, he was on the chopping block to be recommended for dismissal based on lack of aptitude. As I listened to the stories about him, I wondered how he had survived Plebe Summer. His lack of performance consistently resulted in a lot of yelling, screaming, insults, and extra military instruction (EMI). Typically, a midshipman like him would have been gone by the end of the summer. He was obviously determined to stay, and there had to be more to this story. Someone saw potential in him or he would not be at the Academy. As the group discussed recommending him for dismissal, I made a special request. I asked he be placed in my squad and I be

Fair

given a chance to reach him. After several, "Who do you think you are?" type comments, they acquiesced and assigned him to me.

The next day, the squads were announced, and I quickly arranged to meet with each member, starting with the most senior members because we needed to agree on our goals and approach to leading and developing the underclass. I discussed Gibbs with each person. They had all heard of him and were already predisposed to getting rid of him. *Was that fair?* Well, I personally knew how that felt, so I was not going to have this behavior in my squad. I got everyone to agree to work on understanding why a bright young man with outstanding potential was failing at the Academy.

Finally, it was time to meet Midshipman Gibbs. He knocked on the door to my room and said, "Request permission to come aboard, sir?" I glared at him, and he quickly restated the question but addressed me as "ma'am." I told him to come aboard and let him know he was not getting off to a good start. He started to apologize, and I cut him off.

"Is 'I'm sorry,' one of your five basic responses?" I asked.

Rattled by this, he quickly responded, "No, sir!"

I was already starting to regret my decision. When he realized his error, he started to apologize—again. If this wasn't so pathetic, it would have been funny.

Fair

I told him to just be quiet, take a deep breath, and let's start over again. I ordered him to stand at "parade rest"—legs shoulder width apart, hands palm over palm at the small of the back—while I spoke to him. I introduced myself as his squad leader and shared with him the reports I received regarding his performance over the summer. And then I asked him the key question.

"Midshipman Gibbs," I began, "do you want to graduate from the Academy?"

He looked fearfully at me, and said, "Yes, ma'am."

I told him to keep his eyes in the boat, and he returned his gaze to a point directly in front of him on the wall. I then asked him, "*Why* do you want to graduate?"

For the first time since we met, he responded appropriately under pressure. He said, "I'll find out, ma'am."

I then gave him permission to speak freely, disregarding the mandatory five responses.

Midshipman Gibbs gave the standard responses regarding service to country and becoming a career naval officer—the typical *yada, yada, yada* responses routinely given to this question. And then he said something that surprised me. He said he wanted to help develop young men and women to reach their full potential, especially the ones society had thrown away. I looked at him for a moment and thought maybe this wasn't going to be a fruitless effort after all.

Fair

"Midshipman Gibbs," I said, "Well let's see if you're up to the task!" I immediately began to grill him regarding menus, newspaper articles, Brigade stripers, the senior leadership of the Navy, all the rates he was expected to know. To my astonishment, he answered each question correctly and with ease. I was dumbstruck. Beyond not being able to distinguish a man from a woman, his appearance and command of his rates were outstanding.

I was so excited and couldn't wait to bring in my second classman to observe this metamorphosis. I told Midshipman Second Class Jones to ask Gibbs his rates. Jones stepped in his face—about two inches away—and started to ask questions. Gibbs' response? Silence. *Crickets*. He totally choked. I was dumbstruck for a second time in five minutes. It was not that Gibbs couldn't learn his rates. He was unable to recite them under certain conditions. I looked at him like he was insane. The disappointment in his eyes was palpable. I told him to return to his room because study hours were about to commence. After he left, I told Jones what happened. We were determined to find out why he choked, and more importantly, how to resolve this issue.

I observed Gibbs for the next few days, and the pattern didn't change. He knew his rates, but he literally couldn't produce a sound when asked by large, aggressive, white men. This would not do. If I dealt with him in the consistent manner often confused with fairness, I would have screamed and yelled and recommended him for dismissal. But I wanted to try to salvage a future officer who would care about his Sailors and who had come to the Academy

Fair

for that reason. I tried talking to him, explaining no one was going to hit him and there was no reason for that level of fear. More importantly, I explained the Academy could not allow him to graduate if this was to be his response to stress. He couldn't behave this way as a warfare officer in the fleet.

Nothing seemed to work. I talked to my Invisible Friends for guidance and woke the next day with a totally unconventional idea. I asked Gibbs to call his mother. I wanted to talk to her. I told him I was at my wits' end trying to help him and maybe she had some ideas. He gave me permission to speak with her, and I was surprised at her response. She was glad someone had finally called her, and she said I needed to "burst the dam." I respectfully asked for clarification.

"If you can get him to respond *once*," she explained, "he won't have this problem again."

When I asked her how exactly she proposed I do this, she said, "Give him something to be *more* afraid of."

More afraid of than those large, aggressive males? "I have your permission to do this?" I asked.

"I am begging you to," she said.

Well, I knew how to do this! I told Gibbs if I saw him choke again when he was asked his rates, I would give him something to be afraid of. His eyes grew wide. He obviously was not expecting this approach.

Fair

I continued, "If you have any questions regarding what I mean by this…ask around." He hadn't seen anything yet. I was going to make his life a living hell, and he would either speak up or voluntarily leave *my* school.

Apparently, the threat was enough. The next day when he was standing in the hall being questioned by an upperclassman, I again heard nothing. I walked out of my door and down the hall toward him like a woman on a mission. His eyes fixed on me, and he started talking. And with tears in his eyes, he answered all the questions—perfectly. Others came from their rooms to observe this. One asked why he was crying, but he just stared at me, and I returned his gaze with the most menacing, angry stare I could muster. Gibbs never choked again. He performed well in the Fleet and in the private sector.

Would it have been fairer to use the standard conventional approach to dealing with a plebe that didn't know his rates? Or, was it fairer to require he know his rates like all plebes, but to develop a custom approach to assisting him when he faltered? I am glad I chose the latter. I'm sure Gibbs would agree.

Thanks to the lessons of my mother, the one-size-fit-all teacher, and Jeremy, I understood fairness existed in a common ecosystem with consistent and dynamic components. We have to lead individuals, individually. It is only…fair — *No Coincidences.*

24 – "And This Too Shall Pass"

Do you know the phrase, "And this too shall pass," is not in the Bible? This famous phrase—which seems to have originated in the writings of the medieval Persian Sufi poets—is often attached to a fable of a great king who is humbled by the simple words. (Yeah, I was surprised, too.) I mentioned from the outset I am not a biblical scholar, but I have had this quoted to me by some who claimed to be. And each time they said it I cringed. I hated it.

As a youth, I would become frustrated with one or another of my parents' many rules. Home, church, school activities, work, and karate. That was the routine. Anything else required special dispensation only granted after significant groveling—and a full background check and urinalysis of everyone else involved. Not that any of it mattered because I had to be home by ten o'clock anyway! *Ten o'clock!* The other kids were just arriving, and they enjoyed laughing at my predicament. I was, "Daddy's little baby girl who had to do everything she was told."

And they were absolutely right. Although my father was now an upright Missionary Baptist minister, he must have been a scoundrel in his younger days. That's the only excuse I can think of for his utter distrust of the males of our species. To him every boy was a carnivorous beast whose sole purpose in life was to deflower his daughter. And dances—they were "dens of iniquity" where the gyrating bodies of the boys and girls could only result in one thing. Back to deflowering again…

And This Too Shall Pass

Even after I was a senior in high school and the curfew was grudgingly extended until midnight, there were the constant comments about "nothing decent happening after midnight." And my father was posted at the door at 12:00 a.m. Not 12:01 a.m., but midnight. If I was one minute late, it was immediate restriction. I told him he should be a warden. He said, "I *am* the warden…of an insane asylum…" ("crazy house" were his exact words) "…and it's my job to keep the criminals *out*." I guess I was crazy, and every boy was there to molest his little girl.

I couldn't even "take company"—have boys come over to visit—in peace. As we sat on the living room sofa in the "forbidden zone" of the house, I could always hear him puttering around nearby. And to add insult to injury, he would let Sergeant—our very large, very protective, full-bred German Shepherd—into the room. Sergeant was never allowed on the furniture, although he would quietly climb onto the foot of my bed every night and creep down when he heard the morning alarm. Regardless, my daddy didn't know that, so Sergeant belonged on the floor.

This rule was strictly enforced. At least until I had company. Daddy would let him in the room, and Sergeant headed straight for the couch. He positioned himself between me and the boy, and if the young man moved there was much growling and gnashing of teeth. This didn't lead to a very active social life.

Heaven help the poor young man who thought he was going to remove my father's little patient from his asylum for a date. He had to provide identification and a full family genealogy—as if my father had not already had him checked out. The boy was told of the curfew rules, and he would be held personally accountable if I was not returned on time *and* in the same condition as when I left his house. He had a gun he would use to reinforce his point, if needed.

Oh, my goodness! I thought I would lose my mind! And as was typical of any teenage girl under these conditions, I was primed to throw a hissy fit. I thought often about what I would say. I would tell him I was almost a grown woman and I should be able to do as I pleased. That he should trust me to do the right thing. And finally, he couldn't tell me what to do anyway because I would be gone soon, and he would have nothing to say about what I did. (Notice I used the word "thought," but not actually "said." Let me be clear—this reaction was not verbal, nor overly overt. I was not stupid.)

I felt as though it was the end of the world, people were laughing at me, and things would never get better. I felt totally misunderstood. *Sound familiar?* This was probably the common disgruntled state of mind of most children whose parents actively managed every aspect of their social life. I thought he was a tyrant!

One sunny Sunday morning, much like every other Sunday morning, I listened to my father preach from the pulpit. The primary focus of his message was, "And this too shall pass." It was as though a huge lightbulb was turned on, and I realized someday I would be 18, and if I prepared myself I would be able to chart my own destiny. What I currently saw as a life sentence in a maximum-security prison was at most just a stint in a holding cell. I just had to continue to do the right things so I would not only receive a college scholarship, but also become totally independent of my parents.

Maybe my daddy sensed my frustration and his message was to remind me that soon I would no longer be in his house, subject to his rules. Soon, I would be responsible and accountable for every aspect of my life. He also emphasized the only thing permanent in our lives is God, and everything else is in transition. "If we are facing a difficult period," he said, "and remain faithful in our efforts to do God's will, we will not only survive, but be blessed on the other end." I heard every word he said, and although I was encouraged to just try to ride this out as a good daughter, my naturally impatient nature continued to raise her ugly head. I really didn't see the purpose of God taking us through these difficulties. If we were good people, He should just bless us all the time.

As though my daddy was reading my mind from the pulpit, he answered my question. He explained these difficult times were periods of learning and growth. "If we choose to be Christians," he explained, "then we are here to help others as they face life's difficulties, not just to constantly bathe in the lavish blessings promised to the children of God. Even Christ did not do this. How can we help others through their trials and tribulations if we never know any hardship ourselves? Even if we have the right answers, the credibility and compassion that come with experience would be lacking."

Oh…okay, I thought, maybe there's something to this, "And this too shall pass" concept.

And then my daddy said something that totally blew me away. I mean, it should have been intuitive, but I guess I never really thought of it until he said it. Daddy explained we would experience cycles during our lives. There would be difficult times that would pass and the outcome would be based totally on how we chose to transition through the challenges. But they would pass. And then he said, "The good times pass, too." He said for those of us who thought we are on top of the world, that we had it all planned out, that we had lived well and were now basking in our just desserts—this too shall pass. His point was God had to be the focus of all the cycles in our lives. We didn't just need him when times were bad, but also during plentiful times, because no matter what the condition, this too shall pass. If God is at the center, it will all work out for our good. I thought, *Wow. Okay, Daddy, I can handle your tyranny. This too shall pass.*

This was probably the most impactful lesson I took with me to Academy. Understanding "this too shall pass" and how we navigated the journey determines the outcome was pivotal to my perseverance.

In previous reflections regarding my time at the Academy, I shared the highs and lows of this experience. Honestly speaking, it was mostly lows. There is no need to repeat the details of those challenges. Individual experiences and the totality of that journey were more than I could have survived, had I not understood "this too shall pass."

But even more important than the temporary nature of this journey was the significance of *how* I traveled through this period. I did my best not to mistreat people, even when they were cruel to me—at least not beyond what was required to eliminate the threat they posed. I also tried to be available to help people. The Academy was a difficult experience for most of the people I knew. If there was anything I could do to aid them on their journey, I tried to be of assistance. My Invisible Friends were always my navigators. Having said that, I still had "the con"—control of the ship in nautical terms. Free will belongs to all of us. So, I was far from perfect, but I tried.

The transient nature of life and all its experiences shape us into the individuals we are today. As long as we live, we remain a work in progress. Whatever today holds for us, this too shall pass, and this passing will leave us changed. I guess at the end of the final journey, all I can hope for is to hear, "well done."— *No Coincidences*.

25 – What's Mine Is Mine

Sometimes people just don't like you. *Am I the only person who has ever experienced that?* I get along with 99% of the people I meet, but that other 1% can be obsessive in their efforts to undermine me. What is sad is, the feeling is not mutual. Heck, most of the time I couldn't pull them out of a police lineup! I usually find out about their detrimental acts or words when someone starts asking questions about some nebulous event I considered irrelevant. But the person's spin on it is so out of context, it would be laughable if it were not negatively impacting me.

Sometimes this behavior is based on something I did or said. I never intended to hurt anyone, but I could be very direct and quickly move into the "fixer" mode—especially if the solution seemed obvious to me. The person may have just wanted to vent. I learned to just keep my mouth shut unless asked for a solution. But then sometimes it had nothing to do with me, but rather what someone associated with me did that motivated the behavior. (That's always fun. As if I don't have enough of my own mistakes to answer for.) But I think the saddest situation is negative obsession by someone I don't even know, who feels a need to be an obstructionist in my life. Whatever the motivation, I experienced this several times—even as a teen.

My mother was the librarian at my high school and very active in the racial integration planning and execution. Since I was already attending white schools and in a special program with only a few students, not much changed for me. But mirroring community sentiment regarding forced busing, some teachers and administrators had a difficult time with the transition. My mother worked hard to ensure the post-integration learning environment was fair for all students. In 1976, I believe black students represented about 20% of the student body in our school, with white students making up the vast majority of the remainder. There were very few other ethnicities—probably less than 2%. The needs of black students could have easily been ignored, which would have resulted in a tumultuous transition. Instead, it was relatively smooth.

My mother made some enemies as an outspoken crusader for all children. She would tell me about how she would terminate unproductive conversations in the teachers' lounge about specific students. She didn't focus only on the needs of black students, but the entire student body—although she often found herself educating others regarding the needs of black students. She was an old-school teacher who believed in loving students—reinforced with a slap across the butt when needed. (She still managed to get away with that for years after it was prohibited—probably because the students knew she loved them.)

I took advanced classes in high school, and in many of these classes, I may have been the only minority, or one of two. Frankly, I didn't pay much attention to this. There was a special group of highly qualified teachers instructing these classes. One of my mother's detractors was one of these teachers. This teacher saw the environment she had come to love change with the admission of black students, although the class composition for this specific teacher didn't change very much. The accelerated program—which began in elementary school with an ongoing series of prerequisites—was not in place in the black schools. So, I was the only "issue" in my class this teacher had to deal with. The combination of dislike for my mother and her inability to accept change made life difficult for me. This teacher responded very coldly to my questions and often ignored my raised hand. I also felt I never received the benefit of the doubt when grading projects, papers, and tests, especially when compared to other classmates.

I decided, *Whatever!* I was busy trying to make critical decisions for my college future, competing in karate, working, performing duties as part of the student government and NJROTC leadership, as well as supporting church activities. I even managed to win a statewide German competition which included a trip to Germany (which I had no time to take). I was not going to let this ~~old curmudgeon~~ experienced academic professional ruin my remaining time before leaving to pursue the next phase of my life. I performed well enough to get at least a "B"—despite this teacher's best effort—to deter me. I was not at all surprised to receive the two "Bs" from this teacher amidst a sea of "As" in all my other classes. At least it was over—or, so I thought.

Getting ready for graduation was insane. I had accepted my appointment to the Academy and in addition to the local media, I was being contacted by national magazines. Requests for television and radio interviews were also coming in. I found out I was named the salutatorian for my class of 562 students. *I guess my Bs didn't do that much harm,* I thought. As part of the student leadership, we were preparing for the actual graduation ceremony and the different roles we would play. It was all moving along smoothly until my mother told me she needed to talk to me.

As I sat beside my mother on the edge of the bed, she had such a solemn look on her face I wondered if someone had died. She said she received some disturbing news from someone who worked in the guidance offices. The teacher with the problem had lowered my grades on my permanent record in the class. I now had two Cs! It was detected after my records were sent to the Academy. Mom thought my transcripts to the Ivy League schools and NROTC may have been correct. I could tell she was concerned about my response. My mother definitely didn't want me to make a big issue of it because my GPA was still over 4.0 and l got everything I pursued. Maybe she didn't want the person who told her to get in trouble. I guess she felt I had a right to know. Permanent records were always sent directly to the schools. The first time I saw the two Cs was in the summer of 2017. They were circled. It was disturbing to think these grades were discussed as part of the Naval Academy admission decision.

I graduated as salutatorian. And, I received an appointment to the Academy. I also was admitted into every Ivy League school to which I applied. I also received an NROTC scholarship. The timing of this teacher's efforts seemed designed to derail the Academy appointment. But what was mine, was mine, and despite the teacher's best effort, this individual could not change that. I did nothing special except try to be the best I could be—no special plans, no huge savings account, only the willingness to obey and deliver. This was also true of my experience at the Academy.

Sometimes there are challenges in life appearing to be bigger than we are; everything just seems to be going wrong. Then, miraculously, it all works out. I am sure most of us have experienced this. I just believe if I'm a good person, play by the rules, love everyone I encounter (even if they hate me), then I have a destiny that's all mine. No one can take it from me. I know my Invisible Friends have my back.

I know some are tired of me talking about my Invisible Friends. You may even be considering having me institutionalized. But after I take you on this brief journey, you will at least reconsider my proposition.

Okay, let's go. A little—five-foot-seven lightweight—black girl from Aiken, South Carolina shows up at the Academy on Tuesday, July 6, 1976, as the only one of her kind. She has to literally fight her way into her company area. She has to periodically prove she can physically handle all comers. She is kept from studying during the required period. Her grades are lowered. Racial slurs are so common she considers changing her name. She completes her summer cruise on a Yard Patrol Craft not designed for berthing. (Her rack sits directly on the deck above the engines. She is very ill the entire cruise and when it's time to flip her mattress for the next person, it's so heavy with fuel she can't lift it—and she can't understand why her lung capacity seems so shallow.) Many of her grades are lowered for three years. She is attacked and injured by an officer. She endures a complicated new surgery technique, even though she requests physical therapy. She is told she is "government property" and must do as she is told or leave. She drags a straight leg cast around for weeks while her knee heals in a locked-straight position. After weeks of painful therapy trying to bend it, the decision is made to manipulate the knee under anesthesia. (Simply put, knock me out and snap it.) She is left with a painful knee that is still turned inward with a partial range of motion and a limp. And she still has to pass all the swimming and physical fitness tests. And so on…

Are you tired yet? I am. There is more, but let's just stop here. The bright spot in all this was the new battalion officer. He was a black Navy Commander and a pilot. This guy was really cool. Things got better after he arrived. At least he lived on the Yard, and I could visit from time to time. He had a very nice family with great kids I really loved. He was a Godsend. A lot of the negative behavior continued, but at least all of it was not so overt. And as usual, I didn't tell him or anybody else about the situation. Remember, collateral damage?

Although I was not telling my battalion officer every time someone did something to me, he had not reached the rank of Commander in the Navy without having a sense of how difficult things could be. I am sure he had a few stories of his own.

So, I thoroughly believe there were angels working in the background. The angel that put him as my battalion officer. The angel that said I passed the mile run test by a few seconds—swinging a stiff leg and in so much pain I collapsed on the track after I finished. The angel that kept me afloat for all those swimming tests with only one good leg. The angel that ensured I actually received the grades I made as a Firstie, resulting in my being on an honor's list.

I was even Regimental Adjutant for Plebe Summer (second set detail)—a three-striper position. I was a squad leader and also a two-striper on my company staff. I didn't apply for any of these positions. I just went where I was told to go and did the job. I figured no one else wanted to do these jobs. Or, an angel determined if I could survive the incomplete list of obstacles detailed in the earlier paragraph, I deserved these opportunities. It would have been easier to be a midshipman-in-ranks with no other responsibility than enjoying Firstie year and graduating. But it was not about me. Having me visible encouraged some of the underclassman and future midshipmen. If I could do it, they could do it. For whatever reason, all the obstacles placed in my way couldn't stop this from being mine.

And finally, the angel that influenced the medical board to leave the decision to me, whether I commissioned or just graduated. And on May 28, 1980, I graduated and was

What's Mine Is Mine

commissioned as an officer in the United States Navy. From the racial- and gender-based biases of a small southern town to the overt aggression at the Academy, my experiences helped me to recognize no one could take what was truly meant for me. The victories of my adversaries during these small skirmishes didn't determine the final outcome of the war.

So, what's my point? People usually get what they deserve if they are patient, pliable, and prepared. Whether you call it karma, fate, destiny, or the will of God, what happens to us in life is no coincidence. Graduating from the Academy was part of a plan. I am eternally grateful for the people placed in my path to enable this plan. What God had for me, He had for me! — *No Coincidences*.

26 – Closing

The book, *Ender's Game,* by Orson Scott Card is a favorite of mine. Maybe because I can relate to the novel's protagonist Ender Wiggins, who was selected to attend a Battle School responsible for transforming gifted children into military commanders. Ender was bred to perform a very difficult task against a formidable enemy. He had to prove himself along the way by doing things that were against his desired nature. In the end, he defeated the enemy, but was left permanently scarred by the process. I find a quote from the novel quite poignant: "In the moment when I truly understand my enemy, understand him well enough to defeat him, then in that very moment I also love him. I think it's impossible to really understand somebody, what they want, what they believe, and not love them the way they love themselves."

In the novel, failure to communicate caused unimaginable death and destruction. In Ender's world—and at the Academy—unchallenged negative beliefs were the true enemy, and this is what I sought to destroy. Years of learning and preparation as a youth taught me it was not about individuals, groups, race, or gender. I was what they believed me to be, and that formed the foundation of their reality—a reality they valued and were willing to fight to maintain. I also understood their beliefs were important to them, as mine were to me. I had to respect this if I was to successfully challenge these beliefs, the catalysts for the behaviors I experienced at the Academy.

Closing

This understanding allowed me to navigate through the Academy without lingering anger and definitely with no animosity. Like Ender, I understood and loved my enemies. Many people will find this difficult to comprehend, especially after reading this book. This book is not about a series of somewhat sensational events that occurred between July of 1976 and May of 1980. It is about the journey of learning, and discovery based on a solid foundation of preparation and perseverance. The Academy is the source of my sisters and brothers to whom I will always be loyal—even when we disagree. Over the decades many of the people who make up the collages of individuals in this book have apologized or atoned, in some other manner, for their deeds and acts. I forgive them. That's what families do.

Some may question my loyalty based on what I shared in this book. They will consider these experiences to be "family business," not for public disclosure. Again, I understand this perspective, but I respectfully disagree. My desire is that this book becomes a catalyst for discussion—for open and honest communication. This is the foundation for sustainable progress instead of the "appearance" of progress. The Academy is merely the backdrop for the concepts in this book. The message is for a nation that continues to struggle with true freedom and equality that enables all members of our society to share in the American Dream.

My Academy brothers and sisters, rest assured I only shared to the extent necessary to communicate the messages. My

Closing

primary message is that life is an interconnected series of events, that if properly navigated, prepares us for what is to come. "Coincidence is God's way of remaining anonymous" is a prolific quote attributed to several noteworthy figures. For me and my journey, I believe God was very visible, and anonymity was never a part of the equation. My confidence in His presence was—and is—the foundation for my survival.

My secondary message is that we must talk to one another and truly listen. And by listen, I mean attempt to understand one another's perspective and to empathize with each other's feelings. We have to shed the bonds of misinformation and fear that rob us of the opportunity to truly know one another—and just talk. The conversation may be uncomfortable and may unleash a flurry of emotions, but these feelings should never be impediments to openly sharing perspectives and feelings. Without this honest discourse, we will continue with the illusion of progress, that results in total astonishment when certain realities in our culture rear their ugly heads.

My final message is one of love and forgiveness. Not only is the alternative counterproductive—it poisons the mind, soul and body of those consumed by hate and vengeance. "For all have sinned and fall short of the glory of God" (Romans 3:23). If we cannot move beyond our differences and perceived grievances, we will self-destruct. Although not always well executed, this nation was built on a set of values that tied us together for our common good. Hatred and vengeance were not part of this proposition. We must

Closing

work together to sustain our democracy. There are those patiently awaiting its failure. Although I warned of negative behaviors that result in my reflection, "Contagion"—*LOVE* is contagious too.

I love America, and what makes us great far outweighs our "issues." When I hear the National Anthem, I stand with my hand over my heart, and tears well up in my eyes because I understand our freedoms, truly, are not free. We as a united family still have much work to do in our nation and in our institutions. If we have the discussions—and work together—we will reach our full potential as Americans and responsible members of a global society.

And just as I love America, I love my Academy. I continue to be amazed by the caliber of young men and women that are meticulously selected to lead the greatest military in the world. In addition to leading our military, they will lead families, corporations, governments, and occupy the highest positions of leadership in our nation. But like our nation, we still have work to do. The Academy's mission is not achieved by happenstance or "coincidence." It is a well-planned, deliberate undertaking to graduate the best of the best—prepared to lead a diverse nation leveraging the best qualities of all our citizens.

So, let's talk about it — *No Coincidences*.

Addendum

U.S. Naval Academy Officer Leadership Organizational Structure

Superintendent (O-9)
*[oversees all of the U.S. Naval Academy's functions
and is equivalent to a college president]*

Commandant (O-6)
*[responsible for the professional development
of the entire Brigade of Midshipmen
and is equivalent to the Dean of Students]*

Battalion Officer (O-5)
[leads one of the six battalions]

Company Officer (O-3/O-4)
[leads one of the 30 companies]

**U.S. Naval Academy Midshipmen Leadership Organizational Structure
The Brigade of Midshipmen**

Brigade Commander (Midshipman Captain, 6 stripes)

Regimental Commander (Midshipman Commander, 5 stripes)

Battalion Commander (Midshipman Lieutenant Commander, 4 stripes)

Company Commander (Midshipman Lieutenant, 3 stripes)

Platoon Leader (Midshipman Lieutenant Junior Grade, 2 stripes)

Squad Leader (Midshipman Ensign, 1 stripe)

U.S. Naval Academy Midshipmen Class

First Class Midshipmen or "Firsties" (Seniors)

Second Class Midshipmen (Juniors)

Third Class Midshipmen or "Youngsters" (Sophomores)

Fourth Class Midshipmen or "Plebes" (Freshmen)

About the Author

Janie L. Mines entered Annapolis—the U.S. Naval Academy—as the only African American female in the first class of women. She graduated in 1980 after serving in several leadership positions in the Brigade of Midshipmen. She was later selected to participate in the prestigious Sloan Fellows Program, where she earned an MBA from the Alfred P. Sloan School of Business Management, Massachusetts Institute of Technology (MIT).

Janie held management positions of increasing responsibility as a Navy Supply Corps officer and in several corporations, including Procter & Gamble, Pepsi (Frito-Lay), Hershey Foods, and Bank of America. She is currently an independent executive management consultant focusing on Strategic Planning, Change Management, Quality and Productivity, Integrated Business Transformation, and Program Management.

Janie served as the Senior Advisor, Business Process, Senior Executive Service (HQE-SES) in the Office of the Secretary of the Navy. She facilitated Flag Officers and Senior Executive Service leadership in the implementation of Lean Six Sigma (LSS) and the resulting transformational programs across the Department of the Navy. She currently serves on the Defense Advisory Committee on Women in the Services (DACOWITS).

Janie founded and managed a non-profit organization for over 10 years, Boyz to Men Club, Inc, after observing the needs of adolescent boys in the community. Her awards include National Women of Color in Business (award winner), Olympic Torchbearer, Civic Volunteer of the Year, 9 Who Care (award winner for the Charlotte Metropolitan Area), and a South Carolina

Black History Honoree. Janie has served as a member of the Rotary Club International, the Board of Directors of the Founders Federal Credit Union, and the Board of the Springs Close Foundation.

Janie has maintained her relationship with the U.S. Naval Academy throughout the decades. She continues to positively impact the lives of midshipmen and naval officers through her mentorship and ongoing support.

Janie is available for appearances, book signings, and more via her website:
www.nocoincidencesbook.com

Paperback versions of this book are available on www.noconincidencesbook.com